Dear Rich

Happy

Line

Hunting.

Love Guy.

LEY LINES
A COMPREHENSIVE GUIDE
TO ALIGNMENTS

I'm looking forward to the
posted snippets already...
happy days in 2002, love Sam.

LEY
LINES

A COMPREHENSIVE GUIDE TO ALIGNMENTS

DANNY SULLIVAN

PIATKUS

© 1999 Danny Sullivan

First published in 1999 by
Judy Piatkus (Publishers) Ltd
5 Windmill Street, London W1P 1HF
E-mail: info@piatkus.co.uk

This paperback edition published in 2000

The moral rights of the author have been asserted

A catalogue record for this book is available from the British Library

ISBN 0-7499-2017-3 hbk
ISBN 0-7499-2137-4 pbk

Typeset by Wyvern 21 Ltd, Bristol
Printed and bound in Great Britain by
Mackays of Chatham PLC

CONTENTS

*This book is dedicated to the memory of my father,
Daniel John Sullivan*

PICTURE CREDITS

For permission to reproduce copyright material, the author and publisher would like to thank the following:

Plate 1: Daniel Sullivan; *Plate 2*: Daniel Sullivan; *Plate 3*: Detail from *The Prospect Before Us* by the Albion Dance Band from an original painting by William Dudley; *Plate 4*: Photo C. Carr-Gomm, courtesy of Hereford County Library; *Plate 5*: Photo Vivians of Hereford, courtesy of Hereford County Library; *Plate 6*: Daniel Sullivan; *Plate 7*: Daniel Sullivan; *Plate 8*: Photo Alfred Watkins, courtesy of Hereford County Library; *Plate 9*: Tony Morrison, courtesy of South American Pictures; *Plate 10*: Tony Morrison, courtesy of South American Pictures; *Plate 11*: John Palmer; *Plate 12*: John Palmer; *Plate 13*: Daniel Sullivan; *Plate 14*: Daniel Sullivan.

Page 177, Three menhirs at Oppagne: John Palmer; *page 194*, Loanhead of Daviot: Jeff Saward; *page 197*, Merrivale stone rows: Bryan Bing.

While every effort has been made to trace all copyright holders, we apologise to any holders not acknowledged.

ACKNOWLEDGEMENTS

You could say that this book has been 25 years in the making, as during that time many people have inspired and encouraged me to pursue the line of enquiry that led to this publication. Notable participants have been Graham Moss and Charles Dunnett, who first introduced me to the theories of Alfred Watkins in 1974; Tim Whittaker for giving me a copy of *The Old Straight Track* the following year (which I still have); John Michell for *The View Over Atlantis*; Roger Cudby, who encouraged the formation of Gloucestershire Earth Mysteries Group in 1987 which led to my introduction to the Earth Mysteries small press; Philip Burton for his generous support of my Earth Mysteries magazine *3rd Stone* in penurious times; Paul Devereux for his inspiration and belief in me, and for putting *The Ley Hunter* in my hands; Lionel Stanbrook for the idea and his persistence, drive, commitment and help with the planning and construction of this book; and my long-suffering wife Jo, for her patience, determination, the relentless pursuit of a publishing deal, and for wielding a sharp pen here and there when it mattered.

Special thanks also go to John Palmer, Ulrich Magin, Phil Quinn, Jeff Saward, Eugene Zimmer, Brian Hoggard, Laurence Main, Gerald Frawley, Dewi Bowen, Gordon McLellan, Dave and Lyn Patrick, Paul Bennett, Brian Larkman, Michael Dames, Chris Castle, David Olmen, Martin Brennan, Ron Fletcher, Alfred Woodward and Wayne Perkins, for correspondence and contributions here and there, and for doing the work that kept ley hunting alive in its manifold forms over the last 20 years or so, and whose contribution to the subject has formed the bedrock of this book.

Thanks too to John Palmer, Jeff Saward, Brian Byng and Tony Morrison for permission to reproduce their illustrations, and to Mr Robin Hill of Hereford City Library for permission to reproduce material from the archive of the Straight Track Postal Portfolio Club.

INTRODUCTION

My interest in prehistory, and megaliths in particular, can be traced to a casual visit to Stonehenge in 1969. My memory of first seeing the stones appear on the horizon of Salisbury Plain as we approached the site from the main road on that dismal summer afternoon has persisted down the years. While I wandered among the stones (you could still do that in those days) preparations were underway to publish a book that would ignite a popular interest in the mysteries of our prehistoric past. That book was *The View Over Atlantis* by John Michell, the very book that I borrowed from a student colleague five years later as I started out on my academic career at Nottingham University. I became intrigued by the idea of leys and quickly devoured the few books then available on the subject. My friends were equally enthusiastic in those early years and we spent many an hour tracking leys across the Derbyshire moors, making frequent visit to stone circles and eventually spending long hours in Wiltshire dangling pendulums and pointing dowsing rods crafted from wire coat-hangers, over and around standing stones.

Such was my enthusiasm for the ancient sacred sites of Britain that I spent most vacations hitching around the south-west and eventually driving all over the country visiting and photographing as many sites as possible (see Plates

1 and 2). Along with my consumption of speculative literature on leys and Earth Mysteries, this led me to research the subject in some depth for my final year dissertation. That my tutor allowed this on an architecture course still confounds me to this day.

Megalithomania (as John Michell termed it) is a life-consuming passion, and this continued well after my studies had finished. I subscribed to a small publication called *The Ley Hunter* and eagerly awaited its annual summer gathering, or moot, which was held in a different part of the country each year. At these meetings famous faces and big-time authors and researchers would gather, and each year new research and new discoveries would fire me up to get more involved. Eventually I helped found an Earth Mysteries group in Gloucestershire, the county to which I gravitated after university. From that informal group of enthusiasts I launched one of the first local Earth Mysteries magazines, *Gloucestershire Earth Mysteries* (or *GEM* as it later became known). Taking a lead from *The Ley Hunter*, *GEM* organised field trips, its own modest moots, and tracked leys across the Cotswolds with varying success.

Eventually, *GEM* reinvented itself as *3rd Stone, the Magazine for the New Antiquarian*, and its horizons spread to include all aspects of ancient sites, Earth Mysteries, strange phenomena, UFOs, alien animals, crop circles and paranormal phenomena.

During this time I was invited to become assistant editor of *The Ley Hunter* and juggled my time between the two publications before eventually taking over *The Ley Hunter* from Paul Devereux in 1996. In over 30 years of publication the journal has reflected the dramatic changes in the study of Earth Mysteries, from its hippy revival in the late 1960s to its modern day quasi-academic manifestation. Ideas about leys have changed considerably in that time, due largely to the ground-breaking work of Paul Devereux. Not everyone shares his vision, however, and many other diverse ideas, some insightful, some plain crazy, still surface and are pursued enthusiastically by many people. Indeed, a whole new generation of curious folk are eager to uncover the mysteries of the past; people with little or no knowledge of the background and history of ley hunting.

Since the ley revival in the 1960s there have been several attempts to document the history and development of the subject, but I believe no-one has yet summarised the perplexing, challenging and unusual subject of ley lines in an adequately objective and non-prejudicial way. *Ley Lines* is my attempt at a readable, and I hope, open-minded history that embraces a wide spectrum of opinion and gives pointers for a more inclusive approach to a subject that should not focus on the investigations of any one individual.

Dismissed by some as pie in the sky, embraced by others as a magical manifestation of the Earth under environmental stress, or as an eccentrically British form of feng shui, the reasons behind the systematic making of marks in perfect alignment on the landscape have presented a persistent enigma since the discovery of ley lines earlier this century.

This book aims to lay some of the ghosts and settle some of the arguments. It will not tell you exactly what ley lines are or were originally supposed to be; nobody knows that for sure. It does not claim to solve one of the great enduring mysteries of our countryside, but it does provide some answers and insights into the extraordinary phenomenon of the ley line. Not least, it may inspire you to explore the glorious countryside that nowadays so many deny, defile and ignore.

The book also traces the origins of ley hunting, explores and analyses some of the assumptions made over the years as well as the most recent theories for the alignments, and examines those propositions that have sought to explain the mystery by reference to dowsing, crop circles and several other unexplained phenomena. It shows how the original ideas of the measured and modest Alfred Watkins, an Edwardian Englishman who first discovered alignments near Leominster in the early 1920s, remain relevant and appropriate today, and that on the available evidence Watkins should now be re-credited with one of the most exciting, prescient and influential archaeological discoveries of the century.

This is a challenging starter manual for the modern ley hunter, containing 50 examples of leys throughout Europe that can be inspected and analysed by anyone with a good pair of walking boots, a map, a compass, a respect for ancient sites, and an abiding love of the natural environment.

The book also emphasises the unusual strength of the link between verifiable ghost sightings and ancient alignments, and examines the relationship between the 'dead straight' alignment and archaic religious ceremonies, many of which are still observed in some parts of the world today. The discovery of perfectly straight alignments and tracks outside the UK and Europe, in New Mexico, Bolivia and Peru, for example, has rekindled the debate at an international level.

While there may be no precise or easy definition of a ley, landscape alignment still provides us with a perfect opportunity to revive the original enthusiasm and commitment of the ley hunter, and restore the practice of ley hunting amongst all those with a genuine interest in the lay of the land and its ancient secrets. Above all, I hope that reading this book will open your eyes to the remaining wealth and magic of our fast-disappearing rural heritage. As we approach the Millennium and anticipate our place in tomorrow's world, we will be glancing back into the dark even as we gaze into the light. Perhaps by looking along the old straight track we may learn a few lessons for our journey into the next century.

CHAPTER I
THE MYSTERY OF
LEY LINES

At first hearing, the idea that ancient mounds of earth, burial places, prehistoric standing stones and old churches should have been constructed on invisible straight lines stretching in all directions across the face of the country seems quite absurd, but that is exactly what Alfred Watkins suggested when he first made public his discovery of ley lines in 1922. Why should our primitive ancestors have bothered with such incomprehensible feats of surveying and engineering? However hard to explain, the notion that special sacred places are arranged in line with one another over great distances has played on the romantic imagination since Watkins's revelation as he sat in his car at Blackwardine perusing the Ordnance Survey map and gazing across the Herefordshire countryside towards the ridge of Croft Ambrey hill fort. However bizarre ley lines may seem, deep in the human psyche they touch a nerve. They open a door on some almost forgotten sense of order and present us with a view over our increasingly threatened countryside that sees beyond the immediate concerns of farmers, road builders and town planners.

Ley lines, claimed Watkins, criss-crossed the whole of Britain and could be found anywhere by anyone. Among the features to look out for were beacon hills where signal fires once burned, artificial mounds, earthworks, ancient circular moats and old churches built on pagan sites. He asserted that a lost principle linked these ancient waymarkers that often marked the routes of some of our earliest roads and trackways in the centuries before the Romans set foot in Britain. Watkins's ideas formed the basis of his book *The Old Straight Track*, published in 1925, which remains the definitive work on ley lines.

Alfred Watkins provided copious evidence to back up his claim that leys were the remnants of prehistoric trackways, and his followers took up ley hunting with great enthusiasm, forming a club – the Straight Track Postal Portfolio Club – through which to co-ordinate their activities. Their explanations and interpretations of ley lines were many and varied. It seemed the deeper these ley hunters dug into the past the more confusing ley lines became. Not only did they discover long-lost trackways, they unearthed lines of sites pointing to sunrises at significant times in the year, lines of massive earthworks that could never have been constructed for any practical purpose, parallel lines of sites and regular

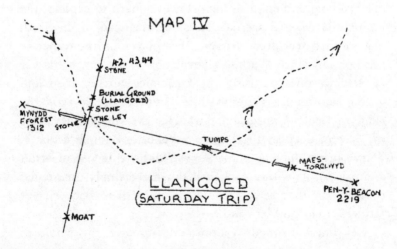

One of Alfred Watkins's hand-drawn maps of leys around Llangoed, drawn for the 1933 Summer Meeting of the Straight Track Club.

geometrical relationships between sites forming giant landscape figures that were on so vast a scale that they were forced to question whether they could ever have been the work of man.

Landscape lines and patterns

Even in the late 1930s, members of the Straight Track Club were suggesting more esoteric explanations for Watkins's prosaic discovery. In 1939, Straight Track Club member Major F.C. Tyler, a colleague of Alfred Watkins, published a pamphlet entitled *Geometrical Arrangement of Ancient Sites* in which he put forward data in support of Watkins's ideas. He noted that many leys shared a common point of intersection; they would converge on the same place, often an insignificant village or site that would never have required such a profusion of tracks. Ley points on these alignments often occurred on concentric circles that could be drawn around the site on the map, and which were spaced at regular and specific distances from the centre. Elsewhere he found leys running parallel for several miles which caused him to doubt that they were primarily used as trackways.

Tyler's conclusion was that the ancient tracks and roads, where they were still traceable, did, as Watkins claimed, conform to the alignments, but more significantly that *the alignments were there before the trackways were established*. The alignments, he said, were 'the remaining index of some great geometrical arrangement of these sacred sites', the nature of which he was unable to specify. Add to this the sometimes impassable ground over which many of Watkins's old straight tracks ran, and the field was opened for a rash of alternative explanations for the ley system.

In the same year, another Straight Track Club member, Arthur Lawton, submitted a pamphlet to the Club entitled

Mysteries of Ancient Man, in which he introduced the idea that ancient sites of the type used by Watkins as sighting points on his leys, formed patterns on the ground with fixed distances and angles. He and Tyler were not alone. A year earlier, Dr Josef Heinsch, working independently in Germany, presented a paper to the International Congress of Geography at Amsterdam entitled *Principles of Prehistoric Sacred Geography*. He spoke of a lost magic principle by which holy sites had been located in the remote past. He claimed the sites were points on the lines of great geometrical figures which were themselves constructed according to certain fixed azimuths (horizontal angles) and to regular units of measurement, all based on simple fractions of the Earth's dimensions. Further, and to some extent in accordance with the principles outlined by Watkins, he claimed that this ancient pattern was still recognisable in the present landscape because of the adoption of pagan holy sites by the Church after the introduction of Christianity into Europe.

As Watkins was formulating his ley theory, another German, an evangelical parson by the name of Wilhelm Teudt, began to construct a fictitious folk history of the German race based upon his study of the famous Externsteine chapel, in an attempt to raise the spiritual consciousness of the German people, humiliated by their defeat in the Great War. He claimed that this rock-cut chapel in one of several naturally occurring giant twisted stacks of limestone in the Teutoburger Wald near Detmold in West Saxony, was a solar observatory, and that 'astronomical lines' linking numerous sacred sites radiated outward from this holy site throughout northern Germany. These lines he called *'heilige Linien'*, or 'holy lines' and their similarity to Watkins's leys are remarkable. Like Watkins, he published his findings in a book, *Germanische Heiligtümer* (*German Sanctuaries*), which inspired others to search out examples of *heilige Linien* and culminated in the formation of a Society of Friends of German Prehistory, a sort of Teutonic Straight Track Club. Like the study of leys, the pursuit of holy lines in Germany died out before the end of the Second World War, and Teudt and his theories were consigned to obscurity.

The post-war ley hunting revival

The outbreak of war may have put a stop to most ley hunting activity, but the mysterious straight lines found new adherents in the 1950s. Once again Alfred Watkins's original and almost forgotten discovery formed the focus for a new generation of free-thinkers posing questions about our enigmatic past that archaeologists and historians were unable or unwilling to answer.

The number of visitors to ancient sacred sites has increased enormously in recent years, and still the questions are asked. How did primitive people drag massive stones miles across country to build monuments like Stonehenge and Avebury? Did they have sophisticated astronomical knowledge? Were they able to communicate with the spirits of their dead ancestors? Could they fly? Were they susceptible to subtle energies within the Earth? Are there secrets to be discovered that could benefit us today? And so on. The one subject that cuts through all these questions is the ley line, touching as it does on all aspects of prehistoric activity, from the building of sacred monuments to the burial of the dead and the uneasy relationship between mankind and the spirit world.

Flying saucers and the straight line mystery

The interest in ley lines was rekindled through an unlikely connection with a new popular obsession – the flying saucer. In 1947, American pilot Kenneth Arnold, flying over the

Cascade Mountains in Washington State, USA, spotted a formation of crescent-shaped shining objects flying at high speed across his line of vision. He later described these objects as moving like 'a saucer skipping across the water'. By the time the story had been reported by the local press his objects had become 'flying saucers' and were about to grip the public imagination on both sides of the Atlantic.

In 1958, the French UFO researcher Aimé Michel published a book entitled *Flying Saucers and the Straight Line Mystery*, in which he proposed the controversial theory that reported UFO sightings in France, when plotted on a

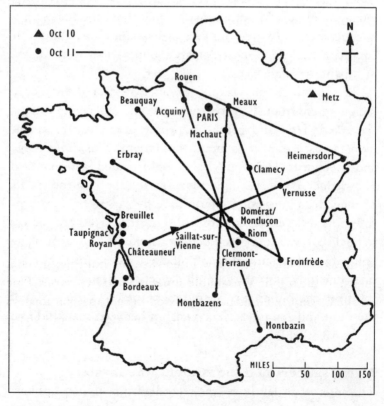

Aimé Michel's map of UFO sightings and alignments in France in 1954.

map, fell into perfectly straight lines. He called this phenomenon 'orthotony', after the Greek 'orthotoneis', meaning 'stretched in a straight line', and the parallels with Watkins's discovery of leys are remarkable. Discredited now and rarely referred to in UFO literature, this unexpected observation was to become the catalyst for a modern revival of ley hunting.

In 1961, Tony Wedd, an ex-RAF pilot living in Surrey, privately published a modest booklet entitled *Skyways and Landmarks*, in which the ideas of leys and flying saucers were brought together for the first time. A melding of French *orthotonies*, Watkins's leys and a love of the countryside led Wedd to the bizarre notion that UFOs used ancient mounds and hilltops as navigation beacons: 'I began to suppose . . . that the saucers' crews knew about the leys', he wrote. In particular he was drawn to one of Watkins's least convincing, but most evocative ley markers: isolated clumps of Scots Pines. There are several atmospheric photographs in *The Old Straight Track* which show mounds and hills crowned with these trees, and it is not difficult to see how these must have played on Wedd's imagination.

Two grammar school boys, both flying saucer enthusiasts and members of Tony Wedd's Star Fellowship (a society whose members believed that mass contact with extraterrestrials was imminent), resolved to revive the Straight Track Club and to encourage new interest in ley hunting, given a boost by the public's insatiable appetite for UFO stories. One of them, Jimmy Goddard, expressed his enthusiasm for leys and UFOs in the magazine *Flying Saucer Review* in 1964:

> 'Could it be that the intelligences behind the flying saucers built the ley markers for navigational purposes, or perhaps in order to find readily a form of magnetic current that is helpful to them?'

Wedd's ideas developed from the claims of alleged UFO abductee Buck Nelson in 1956, who said that flying saucers utilised lines of magnetic current along which they navigated their craft. Fuelled by Tony Wedd's enthusiasm for the res- urrected ley system, Jimmy Goddard and his friend Philip Heselton revived the Straight Track Club in 1962, and in 1965 their newsletter, *The Ley Hunter*, was published for the first time. A key belief at this time was that leys were somehow related to an invisible energy, identified then as 'magnetism', but which would take on a more esoteric char- acter in the next few years.

Lines of force

The idea that there was some other reality behind the ley system, however, was neither new nor exclusively confined to the world of UFOlogy. As early as 1911, a classic work on the fairy lore of Ireland, *The Fairy Faith in Celtic Countries* by W.Y. Evans-Wentz, mentions the folklore of fairy paths or passes along which invisible elemental spirits are believed to travel; he refers to them as arteries through which the Earth's magnetism circulates. This may have been the source for the reference which appeared in the occult novel *The Goat Foot God* by Dion Fortune, in 1936. In it she refers to ancient sacred sites as power centres and sug- gests, without direct reference to Watkins or leys, that they are 'linked by lines of force'.

In his pamphlet on leys, Straight Track Club member Major F.C. Tyler made this curious remark which heralded a revolution in alternative studies of the prehistoric legacy of Britain and beyond:

> 'It appears that there are a number of dowsers
> who have unwittingly detected the consecration
> (of these sacred sites), which gives the same

reaction to the dowsing rod as is obtained from water. This, however, is a suggestion of my own, and I do not ascribe this idea to others. Anyway, it is a romantic one, even if not based on logical reasoning.'

Such ideas might have been consigned to obscure footnotes in history and folklore had it not been for the enthusiastic ley revivalists of the mid-1960s. This concoction of UFO fever, Watkins's leys, dowsing and lines of force formed a powerful and disorientating intellectual environment. One of its key figures was John Michell, probably the most articulate and influential writer on the subject of leys and alternative studies of the past. His articles in the alternative newspaper *International Times* eventually led to the publication, in 1969, of his seminal work, *The View Over Atlantis*, in which he eruditely expounded his inspirational synthesis of UFOlogy, folklore, leys and archaeology, which gave form and focus to the ideas that were to become known as 'Earth Mysteries'.

Earth Mysteries

In his book, John Michell went further than any of his contemporaries, with the inclusion of new material relating to the ancient esoteric and obscure Chinese system of feng shui. In simple terms feng shui was a set of rules for the correct placement of tombs and other sacred buildings in the landscape. The ancient Chinese believed the landscape was a living thing and that subtle forces, referred to symbolically as 'the breath of the dragon', flowed through 'veins' in the earth. These forces had to be found and kept in balance whenever a tomb, temple or house was built. Some places were more auspicious than others and bad luck, financial ruin and even death could befall any person who disrupted the dragon's breath without taking the proper precautions.

Over the centuries, feng shui, or geomancy as it was described by 19th century Christian missionaries to China, developed into a highly complex system of pseudo-science and superstition and has continued to be practised in China, Hong Kong, Taiwan and Singapore to the present day. A westernised version has recently gained popularity in the United States and Western Europe. Michell identified the straight *lung mei*, or 'dragon lines', which were laid out as part of the great imperial palaces, as the Chinese equivalent of Watkins's leys. However the 'veins' in the Earth that were believed to carry the 'breath of the dragon' were anything but straight.

Similarly, through an investigation of the writings of anthropologists on the traditions of the Australian aborigines, he brought to the attention of a new audience the idea of the Dream Time. This was a mythical period in aborigine history, set at the dawn of time when mythological creators or gods emerged from the surface of the featureless Earth and began to wander aimlessly across it. As they did so they carried out the same day-to-day tasks that aborigines do today: they camped, made fires, dug for water, performed ceremonies and other relevant activities. When the Dream Time came to an end the creators marked every place in which they had performed a task or ceremony with a rock, a hill, a watercourse or some other natural feature. Those wanderings across country are preserved in the songs and stories of the aborigine tribes who now inhabit the land. Each tribe has possession of one part of the whole creation myth and the finishing place of a 'line of songs' is where the myths and songs change hands to another tribe and hence form a tribal boundary. Michell infers that these 'songlines' somehow relate to leys and lines of magnetic current, though the non-straight aspect of both the dragon lines and the aborig-

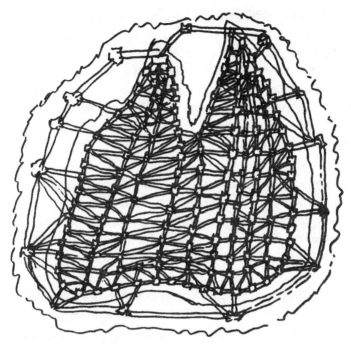

A map of mythic Australia by David
Mowajartai. The square nodes represent
Aboriginal stories and the lines linking each story
are the lines of communication between the tribes.

inal songlines was a matter that wouldn't be fully addressed
by ley researchers for several years.

The impact of *The View Over Atlantis* cannot be over-
estimated. For many it was the first introduction to the work
of Alfred Watkins and it inspired many writers and
researchers to take up the ley cause again in an explosion of
antiquarian interest not seen since before the War. In the
same year, *The Old Straight Track* was republished with a
foreword by Michell:

'The expansion in antiquarian thought, now
taking place, is due in no short measure to the

insight, scholarship and determination of a
provincial visionary, a true Gnostic in that he
preferred the evidence of his own senses and the
voice of his own intuition to the unsupported
assertions of authority.'

The pattern of the past

Shortly before the publication of *The View Over Atlantis*, and
in time for Michell to include mention of it, there appeared
a posthumous work by the dowser Guy Underwood; *The
Pattern of the Past* was to be as influential amongst the front-
line ley researchers as Michell's book was to the general
reader.

In 1939, Reginald Smith, a leading authority on the Stone
Age and Keeper of the British and Roman Antiquities
Department at the British Museum, read a paper to the
British Society of Dowsers describing how, at the centre of
the prehistoric stone circles and earthworks he had tested,
he had found underground streams of water radiating from
what he called 'blind springs': He suggested that sites for
consecration were not arbitrarily selected but dictated by
geological conditions.

These discoveries prompted Guy Underwood to investigate the claims for himself and he spent the greater part of
his life, up until the age of eighty, touring the country
researching for his book. Underwood produced evidence to
suggest that the location of prehistoric monuments and all
the details of their layout and construction were dictated by
the incidence of what he called 'geodetic lines'. These were
similar to the underground streams traditionally located by
dowsing or water divining. By the method of dowsing he
relocated several lost or unknown archaeological features and
proved their existence by excavation.

Underwood proposed that the forces, detectable by dowsing, are a principle of Nature, unrecognised by science, which are generated from within the Earth. These forces, which have great penetrative power and cause wave motion perpendicular to the Earth's surface, can affect the nerve cells of animals and form spiral patterns that are controlled by mathematical laws. He concluded that these natural forces might be an unrecognised effect of magnetism or gravity.

The tracks and roads under which Underwood dowsed his geodetic lines were winding country lanes and footpaths, and although aware of the work of Alfred Watkins, Underwood made no mention of leys in connection with his 'unknown force'. That connection was to be implied by earth mysteries writers during the early years of the 1970s. It wasn't until the middle of the decade that the final connection was made.

While Underwood was formulating his geodetic theory, it was well known amongst dowsers that some points and places were 'polarised' or 'charged' in relation to others. Some of these charges, it was claimed, exist below the ground, but others, not apparently perceived by Underwood, are above it. The first above ground charges were discovered on ancient standing stones, and this line of research was taken up by Tom Graves, a dowser with an enthusiasm for Earth Mysteries, whose book *Dowsing: Techniques and Applications* included some of the developing dowsing ideas about ancient sacred sites. According to Graves, standing stones are polarised in relation to the ground around them and to other stones where they are found in rows or circles.

Graves spent many hours locating these polarities or changes with a pendulum at the Rollright stone circle in Oxfordshire in 1973. He found that the 'charges' on the ring of stones rarely remained static for long. The polarities changed constantly he said, spinning from one stone to another around the ring. This spinning charge would eventually reach a critical level, claimed Graves, at which point the build-up of charge would shoot out tangentially from the ring, following a straight course a few feet above the ground. This line, he said, was detectable as a faint dowsing reaction. The 'energy pulse', as he described it, travelled six miles south-west of Rollright to a standing stone known as the Hawk Stone. Graves called these dowsable lines 'overgrounds' and went on to find several others at Rollright. He suggested that these overgrounds were the 'semi-physical or non physical reality' behind Alfred Watkins's leys.

Earth energies

Graves expanded upon this chance remark in his major work *Needles of Stone*, which followed in 1978. He developed his dowsing ideas into a theory of Earth energy management which he likened to the ancient Chinese practice of acupuncture, only on a planet-wide scale. Standing stones acted as giant acupuncture needles in a vast geographical energy matrix or power system. It would be fair to say that this book alone is probably responsible for the current popular notion of leys as lines of energy and is as far removed from Watkins's original vision as it is possible to get. But is there any reality behind these ideas and theories?

The Ley Hunter magazine enjoyed a brief run in the mid 1960s and was revived in 1969 under the editorship of Paul Screeton, who adopted the mystical interpretation of leys as expounded by John Michell until the editorship was handed over to Paul Devereux in 1976. Devereux was to pioneer the study of leys for the next 20 years. He was, like most other modern antiquarians, a believer in Earth energy line ideas, and it was decided to set up a research effort to investigate the claims of dowsers, mystics and psychics who were talking about unseen and unrecognised forces at ancient places.

The Dragon Project, as it was named, was a wholly

volunteer effort with no formal funding, which set about trying to track down and measure the elusive 'Earth energy' at
the Rollright stone circle in Oxfordshire where Graves had
found his overgrounds. To this end, they employed a series
of electronic measuring devices and encouraged the involve-
ment of numerous dowsers, including Tom Graves, psychics
and sensitives, recording their responses at the site. The
Project was directed by Devereux and the physicist Dr Don
Robins, and spent the best part of ten years at Rollright and
numerous other stone circle sites, tediously monitoring the
sites for hours through the day and night. Once they had
accumulated sufficient data they hoped they might be able
to draw some meaningful conclusions.

Whilst unusual natural energy effects can certainly be
measured and dowsed at ancient sites, the results of the
Dragon Project were not conclusive, and none of the efforts
expended on the Project came any closer to unravelling the
enigma of the old straight track. If leys are not prehistoric
traders' routes and they are not lines of force, what are they?
The search continued.

The world turned upside down

While modern antiquarianism was being popularised in
the underground press, the real revolution in attitudes to
the ancient past was not to be found on the fringes but in
academe itself. The first body blow to received archaeological wisdom came in the form of an article by Gerald
Hawkins in the scientific journal *Nature* which was swiftly
followed in 1965 by the publication of the popular book
Stonehenge Decoded, in which he suggested the unthinkable:
that the builders of Stonehenge had a working knowledge of
astronomy and had built Stonehenge as a 'Stone Age computer' for observing the movements of the sun and moon and
for predicting eclipses.

Two years later, the engineer and mathematician Professor Alexander Thom's meticulous surveys of megalithic monuments attempted to demonstrate the advanced mathematical, astronomical and engineering skills of prehistoric people. He proposed that a universal unit of measure, which he referred to as the 'megalithic yard', had been used in the planning and setting out of megalithic stone circles and stone rows from the Outer Hebrides to northern France. This suggested a level of Neolithic building skill that flew in the face of current archaeological thinking about the abilities of Stone Age man.

The third and final nail in the coffin came in 1967, when Hans E. Seuss compared radio-carbon dates to the chronology of tree-rings from the Bristlecone Pine and concluded that many archaeological dates would have to be radically revised. This 'recalibration' of radio-carbon dating pushed back the accepted dates for the achievements of prehistoric peoples by centuries. The megalithic monuments of Western Europe were therefore deemed to be far older than anyone had suspected, suggesting that prehistoric people were more sophisticated than the accepted image of the 'woad-painted savage' would have had us believe.

Such radical ideas coming from within the academic system appealed hugely to Earth mystics, and the fact that members of the archaeological establishment were as hostile to these incursions as they were to the idea of leys made them all the more attractive.

The great ley debate

Whilst the ideas of Guy Underwood and Tom Graves were enthusiastically taken up by members of the British Society of Dowsers in the late 1970s, other researchers were pursuing the less sensational aspects of ley hunting.

In 1981, *The Ley Hunter* instigated the first serious debate on the viability of Watkins's ley hypothesis with the renowned prehistorian Richard Atkinson, the author of *Stonehenge*, which was, until that time, the definitive account of Britain's most celebrated megalithic monument. In a letter to the editor he summarised the main reasons why archaeologists rejected the ley idea.

Firstly, he said, the ley concept simply didn't fit the picture of prehistoric behaviour and landscape currently held by the archaeological establishment. The idea that ancient man observed and recorded significant astronomical events within their stone monuments was also originally resisted by Atkinson for the same reason, though he eventually relented and enthusiastically embraced the concept. Secondly, he claimed that ley hunters, working from maps alone, did not take into account the distortions inherent in representing the curved surface of the Earth on a flat sheet of paper. Supporters of the ley theory rejected this criticism on the valid grounds that leys were of insufficient length for those types of errors to have any significant effect on a ground alignment. The vast long-distance leys that had been proposed by some enthusiastic ley hunters, however, were certainly open to such criticism, and this is one reason why such incomprehensible alignments were dropped by serious ley researchers and only pursued by those writers and researchers with more faith behind them than evidence.

A classical example of the long-distance ley is the famous St Michael line, first brought to public attention by John Michell. This contentious alignment has been the subject of heated debate for many years. Now firmly entrenched in New Age consciousness due to its repeated publication since the enormously popular *The Sun and the Serpent* by Paul Broadhurst and Hamish Miller, any level-headed discussion about the St Michael line is all but impossible. The alignment is alleged to be the longest straight line that can be drawn across mainland Britain. It starts at St Michael's Mount off Penzance in Cornwall and extends through a series of churches dedicated to St Michael and St George (both dragon-slaying saints), through the Hurlers stone circle on Bodmin Moor, through Glastonbury Tor in the Somerset levels with the ruined St Michael's church tower on its summit, through the megalithic ring at Avebury in Wiltshire and off across country near the ruined abbey of Bury St Edmunds before diving into the sea off the coast of East Anglia.

With lines of this length distortions due to the curvature of the Earth do become significant, so much so that the line can only be made to work either for short sections of the alignment where the map error is small enough to be insignificant, or if the line is widened so much that it takes on the form of a swathe of up to one hundred metres in width rather than a precisely defined line. As a result, the line is only really convincing at the south-western end where the sites cluster over a manageable distance. Keen not to dismiss the St Michael line, authors Paul Devereux and Ian Thompson proposed the term 'geomantic corridor' in their 1979 book, *The Ley Hunter's Companion*. This term was used to explain the phenomenon, suggesting that the line was probably the result of a series of straight alignments set out roughly end to end.

Eventually the argument was neither lost nor won and researchers went their own ways, either rejecting the idea of long-distance leys completely or embracing them within the notions of Earth energies and sacred cosmic landscapes. The latter interpretation reached its zenith in *The Sun and the Serpent*, when the energy dowser Hamish Miller proposed two intertwining energy lines that approximately followed the course of the supposedly straight St Michael line. The idea proved hugely popular with audiences on both sides of the Atlantic and has remained a bugbear to serious ley research ever since its publication in 1989.

Richard Atkinson's third objection to leys was that they

incorporated sites from widely differing eras, which cannot be shown archaeologically to be even approximately contemporary. Watkins originally tackled similar objections by asserting that early Christian churches were often built on the sites of previous pagan shrines. But without excavation it is impossible to claim such a pedigree for all ancient churches and chapels, and certainly not for those built in the medieval period, all of which feature on his and other leys.

One of the first ley hunters to address the problem of mixed marker leys directly was John Michell, whose book *The Old Stones of Land's End* gave an account of his careful study of the astronomical alignments at stone circles in West Penwith, Cornwall, as suggested by the eminent astronomer and scientist Sir Norman Lockyer in the early years of the 20th century. *The Old Stones of Land's End* showed for the first time a deliberately engineered pattern of aligned standing stones, all of which had been erected at more or less the same time. Furthermore, Michell undertook field work in addition to his map work and discovered stones on the alignments that did not appear on the maps, adding further weight to his contention that the alignments were deliberate and planned. In several cases he also established that the stones in a particular alignment were intervisible – a necessary fact in determining that the alignments had been set out by eye on the ground and were not chance occurrences.

Ley lines in question

The accusation that his leys were the product of chance was the major criticism voiced against Watkins. Take any map, said the critics, and you will be able to find alignments of railway stations, pubs, telephone boxes or anything else if you tried hard enough. Watkins's criteria of at least four primary marker points to confirm a ley wasn't acceptable to the sceptics, and this wasn't helped by Watkins's own enthusiasm for alignments that didn't conform to his own rules, many of which he published in *The Old Straight Track* and the later *Ley Hunters' Manual*. The burden of statistical proof fell to the ley hunters who set about the task in the 1970s with some enthusiasm.

Several attempts at a mathematical analysis of leys had been made in the 1950s and 1960s, but it wasn't until 1976 that Pat Gadsby and Chris Hutton-Squire made their famous and impressive computer analysis of John Michell's Land's End survey. Some of the alignments, they said, were better than chance would predict, adding weight to the argument that they were deliberately engineered. However, the analysis and Michell's database were not without their critics. On the surface Michell's survey was very impressive, but detailed analysis of his methods and the range of sites he included in his study revealed a number of flaws in his claims. In particular Michell's critics claimed that many of the stones that he included in his alignments were not genuine prehistoric standing stones but were natural boulders, gate posts or rubbing posts for cattle.

In 1983 the first scientifically considered criticism of the ley theory was published. In *Ley Lines in Question* archaeologists Tom Williamson and Liz Bellamy set about the task of disproving the claims of Watkins and his revivalist followers. In a detailed and aggressive essay they addressed the traditional criticisms of ley theory and attempted to demolish the rather confused environment of much of the Earth Mysteries literature published at that time. *Ley Lines in Question* was a damning indictment, and although Paul Devereux, then editor of *The Ley Hunter*, put up a vigorous defence and found prejudicial flaws in Williamson's and Bellamy's argument, many of his contemporaries preferred not to tackle the issues raised in the book and simply met it with stony-faced silence.

Robert Forrest and Michael Behrend, who defined the techniques for map analysis of alignments, have done by far the best statistical work on leys. It was Forrest who demonstrated that Watkins's original criterion of four points in a row being confirmation of a true ley was statistically not significant. A simulated ley hunt on a 1:500,000 Ordnance Survey map found hundreds of three-point alignments, less than a hundred four-point alignments, two five-point alignments and no six- or seven-pointers. Determined to make or break the case one way or the other, Forrest was asked by ley hunters Paul Devereux and Nigel Pennick to test his methodology on a selected number of leys that had been found and surveyed in the manner set down by Watkins. The results were inconclusive, the leys coming out equally split between deliberate and chance alignments.

In *Ley Lines in Question*, Williamson and Bellamy claimed a victory. Leys, they said, were simply the result of random chance alignments. Not everyone is convinced by their argument, but while they didn't destroy the ley idea completely, they certainly made serious ley hunters take a close look at their methods and forced them into more accurate and thoughtful map and field work. It also prompted a reassessment of the whole ley idea. From Watkins's simple observations in the field, ley hunting had developed into two distinct camps – the energy line dowsers and the statistical ley hunters. However, a third way was already emerging.

Spirit lines

In 1989 Paul Devereux and Nigel Pennick co-authored a weighty volume entitled *Lines on the Landscape*. In the aftermath of the Dragon Project and the failure of statistics to prove the ley case, they decided to get back to basics and re-examined the evidence for the archaic landscape line in order to shift the emphasis from energy line ideas back to a research-based approach. In the 1970s Pennick had been responsible for unearthing and republishing the obscure writings of individual alignment researchers in Britain and Europe and had researched medieval alignment practices in Britain. Alongside a detailed history and an analysis of current information, the authors now discussed alignment practices in the New World, recent archaeological discoveries, and a re-assessment of known prehistoric linear features in the landscape.

The book was a *tour de force*, but was almost totally ignored by modern antiquarians whose interests, by the late 1980s, had been captured by the more accessible and popular ideas of New Age writers. The once self-contained world of Earth Mysteries was slowly splintering into different factions, embracing modern paganism, the occult, New Age ideas of self-improvement, and the more sensational and immediate areas of crop circles and UFOlogy.

The closing pages of *Lines on the Landscape* hinted at a revolution in ley studies that would herald a new chapter in the study of ancient alignments. What Devereux and Pennick had found was that wherever the straight landscape line occurred, and where it did not have any obvious utilitarian function, such as a road, a boundary or an urban street pattern, it appeared to have a religious significance. They picked up on traditions associated with old straight tracks and roads where obscure ceremonies still survived, and where pilgrimages and processions still took place. The key theme connecting them all appears to be a belief in spirits, both of the Otherworld and of the dead, and a preference for travelling along dedicated 'spirit paths'. These ideas, which had originally surfaced in the correspondence of the Straight Track Club, and which had been discussed by John Michell as early as 1975, had become lost in the excitement and enthusiasm for Earth energies and would prove to be a turning point in the development of the ley idea.

In the following chapters we will examine in more detail the numerous theories that have been put forward to explain, support and resist the enigma of the straight landscape line – Watkinsian ley lines, astronomical alignments, paths of energy, processional ways, old straight tracks, old winding tracks, 'terrain oblivious lines' (as one archaeologist described the straight lines he researched), funeral paths, death roads, corpse ways, spirit lines, or the flightpaths of the gods. Some of these ideas are clever, some are just plain crazy, but each sheds light on a phenomenon that after 75 years still begs an explanation.

CHAPTER 2
ALFRED WATKINS AND
THE FIRST LEY HUNTERS

A ny sensible discussion about the phenomenon of ley lines
would be impossible without re-examining the theories of
Alfred Watkins, the discoverer of leys (see Plate 5). Somewhat forgotten by modern ley enthusiasts, particularly in
Germany and the USA where the dowsing of energy lines is
taken very seriously, Watkins's book, *The Old Straight Track*,
covered a lot more than the assertion that ley lines are invisible straight lines linking ancient sacred sites. He discussed
geography, folklore, place names, astronomy, history and
symbolism, and made a valiant attempt to define the technical aspects of leys: their orientation, how they were originally
surveyed and the practicalities of ley hunting in the field and
on the map. The writings of Watkins's enthusiastic contemporary followers in the Straight Track Club also contained a
wide variety of speculations on the nature and properties of
ley lines, and afforded insights into ideas that were to resur-
face in the post-war ley hunting revival. In addition they have
shaped today's popular idea of ley lines and foreshadowed
some of the latest ideas and thinking on the nature of the
straight landscape line. It is with this original rich diversity
of free-thinking that we begin our investigation.

Despite the current proliferation of theories, the documentary origin of modern ley hunting appears to begin
with a seemingly innocuous paper delivered in September

1921 to a handful of members of a local natural history society, which actually concealed a revolutionary discovery. It claimed that prehistoric people had laid out the ancient countryside in a system of dead straight tracks linking prominent hilltops with alignments of earthern mounds, moats, ponds and standing stones.

Alfred Watkins's Woolhope Club Lecture to a group of Hereford citizens was the modest beginning of a theory that has fascinated and intrigued people ever since, and may yet prove to be the discovery that changes our perception of prehistory and our understanding of life and society several thousand years ago. Alfred Watkins indicated that he was under no illusion about the scepticism that would greet his conclusions. He was already concerned that he would not be taken seriously and stressed repeatedly that this was no theory, it was a genuine discovery.

Three months earlier, on 30 June 1921, he had been driving along a road in Blackwardine, then a small village close to Leominster (now virtually disappeared). Attracted no doubt by the nearby archaeological investigation of a Roman camp, he stopped his car to compare the landscape on either side of the road with the marked features on his map. While gazing at the scene around him and consulting the map, he saw, in the words of his son, 'like a chain of fairy lights' a series of straight alignments of various ancient features, such as standing stones, wayside crosses, causeways, hill forts, and ancient churches.

He realised immediately that the discovery had to be checked from higher ground:

> 'I followed up the clue of sighting from hilltop,
> unhampered by other theories, found it yielding
> astounding results in all districts, the straight
> lines to my amazement passing over and over
> again through the same class of objects, which

I soon found to have been practical sighting
points.'

The vision came to him 'like a flash', and the moment has
since been celebrated in a rather stylised picture, (see Plate
3) and by other enthusiastic commentators as a mystical
vision (which the ever-methodical and practical Watkins
would certainly have indignantly denied). His excitement
was none the less palpable, and he lost no time in returning
home to test his notion by referring to the more detailed local
maps. The line he saw can still be seen in spectacular fashion
from the top of the Iron Age fort at Croft Ambrey to the
north-west, and at Risbury Camp some 20 miles to the south-
west, along a line now represented by various small roads
and paths, including the ancient trackway known as Croft
Lane. The Blackwardine Ley (see Directory of Ley Lines:
Blackwardine Ley) represents the first discovered ley line in
modern times.

Watkins was not the first man to notice alignments at
ancient sites, but he was the first to propose that alignments
existed all over the land, and, crucially, to give them an
appropriate name. He chose to call them 'leys' because of the
frequency with which this Saxon place name occurred along
them. Watkins expanded and edited his Woolhope Club
Lecture, and his own photographic equipment company co-
published it with the London publishers Simpkin, Marshall,
Hamilton, Kent & Co in 1922. Entitled *Early British
Trackways, Moats, Mounds, Camps and Sites*, it added some
linked material on tracks, alignments and place names to his
original lecture.

'It is necessary' wrote Watkins, in a phrase that is even
more appropriate today, 'first to clear the mind of present
ideas of roads from town to town, or with enclosed hedges,
also of any assumption that orderly road planning was introduced by the Romans... Presume a primitive people, with

few or no enclosures, wanting a few necessities (as salt, flint flakes, and, later on, metals) only to be had from a distance. The shortest way to such a distant point was a straight line, the human way of attaining a straight line is by sighting, and accordingly all these early trackways were straight, and laid out in much the same way that a marksman gets the back and fore sights of his rifle in line with the target.' To these indications, one might add that 70 years later it is also necessary to clear the mind of commercial development, town planning, leisure interests and the use of the natural environment.

Watkins spent the following three years consolidating his ley theory. He travelled extensively in his home county of Herefordshire, photographing sites and accumulating an impressive collection of data. Much of his working life, as a travelling representative for his family's business, had given him an intimate understanding of the county, its people, customs and folklore, and his practical knowledge of photography gave him the ability to spot significant features in the landscape that might have been lost to the untrained eye (see Plate 8).

Watkins was a pioneer, and much of the charm of his books derives from his evocative photographs of lost Herefordshire sites; his observations and ideas were bred out of his personal experience and can be said to have been shaped by it. Consequently his explanation for the ley phenomenon was as utilitarian, basic and down-to-earth as the man himself. Watkins concluded that the alignments of prominent hills and the ranks of minor mark points between them represented the routes of prehistoric traders, carrying salt and pottery, amongst other goods, across a trackless, ancient wilderness.

Watkins indulged in considerable speculation about word derivations, finding significance in the terms 'lane', 'lay of the land', 'glade', 'lee', 'leigh', 'lake', and almost every place name that ended '-ley' or '-ly', of which there were many in the immediate vicinity as there are many all over England. Other place names associated with leys included words for salt (Wick, Wich, Whit and White). Watkins claimed to have found several 'salt leys', indicating support for his original theory that the ley system was intended as a way of mapping routes to mines and other natural deposits, as well as to markets. Similarly, Watkins's knowledge of the ancient pottery at Whitney near Hereford, led him to explain that the numerous place names involving the word 'Red' related to clay. He also claimed that place names with the word 'Black' were linked to iron, 'Knap' with flint chippings, and 'Tin' or 'Tinker' with flint flakes. Watkins assumed that place names including the word 'Tot', 'Dod' or 'Toot' would have been accepted sighting points, having been 'tumps' – small mounds of earth, generally on hillsides or near summits whose purpose had not previously been understood.

In a section confidently entitled 'Proof', Watkins stated that the facts could be verified using an Ordnance Survey map and a ruler. He invited readers to mark a ring around all the ancient earthworks, churches, castles, wayside crosses, crossroads or junctions bearing a place name, named ancient stones, traditional tree place names (such as Gospel Oak) and all legendary wells (such as Holy Well).

He then suggested sticking a pin into an undoubted sighting point, placing a straight edge against it and rotating it until several of the ringed features lined up with it. He said that fragments of ancient roads and footpaths and some modern roads are often found to line up along the straight edge.

The confidence of these words is surprising today; a renewed effort of imagination needs to be made not just to conceive of the countryside a few thousand years BC, but to appreciate the physical situation of the English countryside in 1921. Land prices were very low, even in the vicinity of important provincial towns such as Hereford; there was scarcely any commercial development of rural areas outside towns; and with the exception of mining areas, the contours of the British countryside were much the same in 1921 as they had been for thousands of years. It is an unhappy coincidence that much of the physical evidence for ley lines must certainly have existed at their re-discovery in 1921, but had virtually disappeared within three generations. This makes ley hunting today a difficult and frustrating process; what could be discovered then was not retained and does not survive now. In 1921 Watkins was even able to write that:

'If you travel along the actual sighting line you
will find fragments of the road showing as a
straight trench in untilled land, although these
are few and far between, as the plough
obliterates all.'

The plough and the bulldozer have in the last 80 years removed most of the clues, and only a tiny percentage now remain. The fact that there is still some evidence of the ancient tracks in Britain may be due in large part to the common law system that ascribed natural and irrevocable rights of way throughout England and Wales. This legal heritage has preserved much, and incidentally provides an excellent example of why the efforts of landowners to alter or change such historic pathways should always be resisted.

Watkins also broached the issue of the origin of the leys. Who first thought of them? Who constructed them and why? 'Now comes surmise,' he noted: trained surveyors – the ley men – made the tracks, and, more importantly, the landscape marks that delineated the tracks, in order to assist people in locating local resources. Leys, he assumed, were initiated as markers for trade routes some time between 1000 BC and 5000 BC. However, the ley men may have been or become a learned and priestly class through the practice of their craft;

perhaps they were also bards, astronomers and soothsayers, accredited with magical capabilities.

In 1922, the year of publication, Watkins was already 66 years old, and in his 'Endword' to the book he expressed the hope that he was to repeat often over the remaining 12 years of his life: that others would carry on what he had started.

Early British Trackways was fundamentally a work in progress. In places it betrays signs of impatience, as if its overenthusiastic author was trying to get the short manuscript finished as quickly as possible so that he could return to his field research. One can imagine Watkins breathing a heavy sigh of relief when the manuscript was published. Some of the arguments leading to the conclusions are uncharacteristically overpresumptive; Watkins corrected this in his next book and also observed that *Early British Trackways* was a 'somewhat breathless production with many constructional faults and a few crude speculations on place names'. Nevertheless, he had placed the first marker, and this allowed him to take stock and work on improving the evidence, to go on to a more considered and practical phase of work, and above all, to get back out into the field. For him the subject manifested continuing revelations, and almost every day he must have seen evidence that would have led him to refine and improve many of the assumptions contained in his first work. He worked hard on his discovery over the next four to five months, and this work became the basis of *The Old Straight Track*, in which he expanded, expounded and encapsulated the ley line discovery. He also quietly dropped some of the more imaginative presumptions contained in *Early British Trackways*.

Watkins was no mystic; he was a man of extraordinary energy and commitment, especially to the buildings and by-ways of his beloved Hereford. Born into one of the wealthier local families, he spent much of his life assisting with the family brewery and milling concerns, which occupied a fine site in the centre of the town. His passion was photography, and he was a noted inventor of photographic equipment, even creating a company to market the products he designed. One of these, a light meter, was in general use by many photographers and by the British Army until the mid-1960s. He also served as a local councillor, espoused the Liberal cause, and was an early and enthusiastic supporter of women's equality, successfully proposing that women by allowed to join the Woolhope Club. But most of all he was a committed preservationist, and with his camera took hundreds of pictures of his native town and its surroundings, especially when and if he heard that any major building works or excavations were being planned. He was frequently to be found at building sites, methodically taking pictures of the scene, especially of trenches and holes dug for the purpose of foundations, before they were sealed up, built upon, and, for archaeological purposes, lost.

The Old Straight Track was published in 1925. It was a huge book, copiously illustrated (often with Watkins's own photographs) and painstakingly written and referenced. 'My main theme', he stated in the Introduction, 'is the alignment across miles of country of a great number of objects, or sites of objects, of prehistoric antiquity'.

Watkins began the book by concentrating on man-made mounds, which he believed to be the most promising candidates for genuine sighting points. Excavations that had been taking place in the previous two decades had revealed that most of the mounds in Britain were pre-Roman. This was most welcome news for Watkins, who took great pains to warn readers that his subject was not the Roman occupation of Britain, still less Roman roads. Mounds also had the advantage of remaining unaltered down through the ages, unlike the tracks that often linked them. Mounds were also often found on or near a watershed or ridge of hills, and presented obvious sighting points in the area around them. Many were aligned. Watkins finishes the section on mounds by refining the discovery.

There is no doubt, he says, that these alignments are man-made. Many of them stretch for long distances across country and the only way they could have been laid out is by sighting from the top of the highest available hill – hence the occurrence of the natural peak in the alignment. The trained eye, he says, in the unpolluted air of prehistory could have picked out a distant hill peak 60 miles away and the many intermediate hill ridges in between. These later became the sites for mounds and mark points along the sight lines.

Watkins then turned to mark stones. Mark stones then, as now, were often used to depict a path or track, and any surviving lines of such stones would seem to provide excellent evidence of an archaic path, as the stone rows on Dartmoor and at Carnac in northern France clearly indicate. The loss of such stones since the 1920s has been enormous, however, and many of the mark stones mentioned in *The Old Straight Track* can no longer be located. Most have been destroyed or moved during road-widening schemes, making the modern ley hunter's task particularly difficult.

Watkins also suggests that mark stones were planted near to sighting mounds to indicate the direction of a ley, in other words to provide an indication of the direction in which to make a sighting. They were also frequently put at the crossing point of two leys, and are therefore sometimes to be found at present-day crossroads, often in the form of a Christian or Celtic cross. Watkins cites the example of the Yazor Ley as a ley involving mark stones (see Directory: Yazor Ley). Particularly prominent stones were sometimes called 'King Stones', and many were used as the meeting place for medieval open-air courts or local debating places known as moots. There is no reason to suppose that such stones had any less significance before these times.

The Old Straight Track also covered sighted tracks, water-sighting points, mark trees (particularly the Scots Pine), and notches in hills. The sight notches were of particular importance as they resolved the problem of how to stay aligned from vale to hill. Watkins noted several of these near Llanthony Abbey in the Black Mountains. He went on to investigate leys at hill forts and other ancient camps, claiming that the tracks in question often preceded the camps; in many cases the outline of the camp could be determined by reference to the existing trackways.

Watkins always maintained that leys ran between what he called initial sighting points, that is from one prominent hill to another. Sometimes they ran from a holy well or standing stone to a hill or vice versa. All the markers between these initial points would invariably be artificial and laid out by the ancient surveyors. Watkins also found several examples of old straight trackways running up the sides of hills or as hollow linear depressions across unploughed meadows and orchards. Often the old trackways can be seen at certain times of the year when variations in the vegetation show up as ghostly shadows of a former path. Watkins was without the benefit of aerial photography in his day, and many linear and other archaeological features have been discovered by this method in recent decades. Among them are the cursus monuments, which have been shown to contain numerous alignments to prehistoric barrows, standing stones and ancient churches.

Again Watkins returned to the difficult issue of who laid out the tracks and why they did so. In a series of revised conclusions about the ley men, he pointed out that the planning and construction of the tracks was a highly skilled job, needing a considerable number of workers who would have had to work under expert direction. The directors of such mass labour would have been politically significant people, constituting a distinct class set apart from the rest; place names are forwarded as evidence, chiefly the names 'Cole', 'Dod', and 'Black'. 'Cole' turns up in an unusually large number of place names in England, and Watkins correctly challenges the reader to reflect on why there are so many more farms called 'Cole', 'Coleman' or 'Coleshill' than 'Jones', 'Smith' or 'Williams'. Watkins's conclusion is that the 'Coleman' directed the construction of leys, often tended the beacon fire, and may even have provided the origin of 'Old King Cole' as described in the nursery rhyme. Similarly, the 'Dodman' was the surveyor who used a pair of sighting sticks as a basic theodolite for the sighting of the leys. Watkins quotes an archaic meaning for 'dod' as a 'stalk, staff, or club' (*New English Dictionary*). The Dodman, said Watkins, is best represented by the Long Man of Wilmington, at which site there is a particularly good example of a ley line (see Directory: Wilmington Ley). The word 'Black' also intrigued Watkins, and he showed that the name occurs on leys and ancient trackways. It is described by the *New English Dictionary* as a 'word of difficult history' also associated with 'shining, white or pale', explaining the derivation of words such as 'bleach' and 'bleak'. Revising the opinion he gave in *Early British Trackways* that the word 'Black' denoted the iron worker or charcoal carrier, Watkins re-ascribed the word to the person who minded the beacon lit on hilltops to mark the ley.

The prehistoric purpose of a beacon fire was to act as a guide; its extensive use as a warning symbol was a medieval application. Watkins believed that its first use was to fix the point of seasonal sunrise as a basis for creating a ley. In planning a track, the beacon was used as a basis for sighting points, and 'beacon hills' are frequently found at the beginning of leys. A beacon fire on a lofty hill could be seen from all around. Watkins's research suggested that the actual leys sighted from a beacon often crossed a stream or pond because the fire of the beacon could be seen reflected in the water in the precise line of the ley. Watkins knew this imaginative finding to be controversial, but stressed that excellent evidence exists for it. He found the word 'Flash' in the place names of such stretches of water aligned on leys, and pointed to the literary evidence of Kipling and Bunyan, who both refer repeatedly to roads leading direct from a beacon to a ford.

Despite the accumulation of a vast body of evidence – archaeological, factual and anecdotal – and his meticulous attention to detail, *The Old Straight Track* was universally ignored or derided by the archaeological establishment of the time, a situation which still persists to this day. In the 1920s, the accepted view of prehistoric Britons was that they were ignorant woad-painted savages to whom the precise science of land surveying would have been unthinkable. It would be 30 years before Professor Gerald Hawkins analysed the stone alignments at Stonehenge and proposed that it was a sophisticated astronomical observatory; before Professor Alexander Thom accurately surveyed prehistoric stone circles from the Outer Hebrides to Brittany and proposed that they were laid out to precise geometric patterns using a consistent unit of measurement, the megalithic yard; and before radio-carbon dating pushed back the construction dates of prehistoric monuments in Britain to centuries before the building of the Egyptian pyramids. From that moment the established archaeological view of prehistory was turned on its head. Had he lived to see it Watkins would have felt vindicated. In the stuffy 1920s, however, any suggestion that ancient Britons were capable of anything other than subsistence living was met by archaeologists with accusations of heresy. Thus it was that O.G.S. Crawford, then the editor of the respected *Antiquity* journal, refused to carry a paid advertisement for

The Old Straight Track when it was published, and did not review the book either.

That such an idea could have surfaced in Edwardian England is a testament to Watkins himself. A tireless and constantly active man, he had, before his 'revelation', given numerous scholarly papers to the Woolhope Club and published books and pamphlets on subjects as diverse as pigeon houses, Herefordshire place names, architectural history and archaeology, old Herefordshire crosses and bee-keeping, as well as photographing and cataloguing the minutiae of Herefordshire country life.

From this detailed and diverse knowledge came the self-confidence and conviction for Watkins to propose a revolutionary theory about the activities of prehistoric people. He saw life in his slow-paced surrounding landscape as a continuum, and believed that the way of life of country people in his day, unchanged for generations, was directly descended from the activities of ancient country people. In *The Old Straight Track* he says: 'The wayfarer's instructions are still deeply rooted in the peasant mind today, when he tells you – quite wrongly now – "You just keep straight on".' Secure in his beliefs, he had no intellectual difficulty in proposing his ley hypothesis to an archaeological establishment whose concerns were far removed from first-hand and intimate experience of a landscape, its traditions and its people.

Flying in the face of established belief and 'unhampered by other theories' as he put it, Watkins set about the task of overturning the accepted view of prehistory with a commitment and attention to detail that characterised all other aspects of his working life. That he was to be proved right, in spirit if not in fact, is a testament to his vision.

Watkins's memory is preserved in Hereford where his reputation was never sullied by the poor reception from the archaeological establishment. He was a prominent businessman; an amateur archaeologist of repute who provided much of the basic framework for archaeological research in Herefordshire in the following decades; a photographic innovator and inventor and a leader of public opinion in Hereford. His great achievement, the discovery of leys, may have been flawed on several levels, but he nevertheless recorded invaluable information from a landscape that is now lost to us and his work contains clues which, as we shall see, may lead to a better understanding of ancient alignment practices and our relationship, and that of prehistoric man, with the landscape. In his own words: 'Out of the soil we wrench a new knowledge of old, old human skill and effort, that came to the making of this England of ours.'

The first ley hunters

Although *The Old Straight Track* was ignored by the archaeological establishment, it promptly became a popular bestseller. It also stimulated the creation of the Straight Track Postal Portfolio Club (see Plate 4). The Club was a remarkable phenomenon, characterised by an enthusiasm and commitment difficult to imagine today, given the inevitable delays implicit in using the postal service. It was fully operational within two years of the publication of the book, with a mission to promote and extend Watkins's work.

Brilliantly organised, the Club was essentially a round-robin collective and co-operative research project with over 40 subscriber-members whose articles, discoveries and notes were circulated to all other members of the Club. The rules instructed the members to pass the Portfolio on within five days of receiving it, and there was a highly organised system of gummed stickers, postcards and printed notepaper to help the exchange of ideas and theories. As befits the manners of the time, the written (sometimes typewritten) exchanges were polite and tolerant, and although there were occasionally sharp remarks and energetic responses, even these seem mild-mannered, however barbed. F.G. Roe, wrote Alfred Watkins in one dry note, 'is too angry to be truthful'.

The ever-logical Watkins, careful, stern and practical as he was, was aware that his ideas were controversial. 'As an old investigator and inventor I know that surmise and imagination are absolutely necessary in the first stages, and it is a mistake to sneer at these factors as being weak in themselves.' All this 'surmise' was therefore leavened by solid down-to-earth advice, as in Watkins's famous *Advice to Ley Hunters*, much of which holds good today. He insisted that a ley should be exactly measured – it had to be straight, not just somewhere near; a ley should also not be taken as proved with less than four good mark points. Finally, he cautioned against two dangerous subjects: early religion and place names. These observations hold up well today, although it can scarcely be claimed that Watkins followed them. In Portfolio 7, Watkins urged his colleagues to pick up a spade and dig for evidence. This was a time when it was not necessary to go through a complicated process of obtaining permissions and licences to excavate; amateur and private excavations, perhaps unfortunately, were commonplace in Britain until well after the Second World War. Watkins pointed out that it would be virtually impossible to find the original track on the surface of the ground: 'Old street levels in old cities . . . are now six or seven feet below the present surface.'

The Straight Track Club appears to have been set up on the initiative of Barbara Carbonell against the background of hostility and suspicion from the archaeological establishment. A Dr Clay wrote that Watkins was 'ignorant of the first principles of the science of archaeology'; however the words only served to unite the Straight Track Club members in an early defence of their mentor. Club members had a range of occupations, although all must have been relatively well-to-do as the annual subscription to the Club was substantial, at £6. All members appear to have been keen amateur historians; there was a rear admiral and several army officers, lawyers, architects, engineers, local government officials, senior clerks, chaplains and curates. There were also, perhaps unusually, several women members. Many members were themselves archaeologists and antiquarians, some of whom contributed regularly to mainstream journals such as *Antiquity*.

Above all, the Straight Track Postal Portfolio Club seemed to have been a great excuse for days out. Picnics and rambles were held at interesting places, and by all accounts people enjoyed themselves enormously on these excursions. R.J. Wilkinson, writing in *The Scouter* after being urged to introduce scouts to the theory, declared that ley hunting has the power to turn any country walk into a thrilling adventure. This has to have been one of the main reasons for the early enthusiasm of the members, and still provides as good a reason as any for ley hunting.

Within a couple of years, the tone of the correspondence between members gradually became less in awe of Watkins and began to question his key discoveries. Ley lines continued to be found and described, but increasingly some correspondents became unhappy about the apparent lack of explanation for their existence. In Portfolio 8, Major Tyler, the Club's Secretary, first put into writing what Watkins seemed ready to concede, that trade routes could not have been the only reason for the construction of straight tracks; they were 'communications for all purposes of social need'. Tyler also spent some considerable time trying to make fit a theory that alignments could come in two-dimensional forms, such as squares, triangles and parallelograms. Yet it seemed that however they were researched, the sheer paucity of evidence ensured that the alignments were keeping their secrets, and many correspondents simply became frustrated. Watkins, too, tacitly began to share this frustration, and referred less and less to the term 'ley', but the first overt sign of scepticism came from A.H. Mackmurdo, who nevertheless expressed himself with a politeness and subtlety characteristic of the Club's membership:

> 'The hypothesis of the Straight Track, as first envisaged by Mr Alfred Watkins, may possibly upon further experience be found wanting. But at present it holds its own as an explanation of the diverse facts under observation better than any other yet offered; it is one that satisfies both on knowledge of man's past and our own sense of logical fitness.'

Furthermore, while all the members had subscribed to the Club on the basis that Watkins's original discoveries needed to be supplemented and developed, there was very little consensus about the objectives. Plenty of ley lines had been found, but still there seemed to be no evidence leading to an understanding of why they were created. Notified ley lines became longer, more difficult to understand or locate, and more unlikely – one was even proposed that extended between Land's End and the Norfolk Coast, with over 250 mark points; many were also posited that were nowhere near straight.

After 1930, the septuagenarian Watkins still took an active part in the Club and contributed several influential papers of his own, but it would seem that he was increasingly prone to silence when called upon to give an opinion, certainly when he disagreed with contributors. It was as if he were watching the slow deterioration of his initial discovery, and had become sufficiently sceptical himself as to seem almost resigned to the confusion and lack of focus into which the Club was moving. It is true that his advancing years may provide the explanation for his diffident approach, as well as his strong conviction that others should carry the subject forward.

In Portfolio 15, something approaching mutual hostilities seemed to commence, as Major Tyler strove to keep a focus within the correspondence, much of which amounted to bickering over what truly constituted a straight line. John Simpson wrote: 'Do let us sink this obsession of the true alignment'. Major Tyler's riposte was along these lines:

> 'If we abandon the true alignment, then we abandon the whole idea. No alignment can be in existence except a true one; it would be a contradiction in terms to use the term thus loosely . . . The alignment is the whole basis of the straight track theory and we cannot abandon it.'

The Straight Track Postal Portfolio Club was a prime example of voluntary commitment; nobody enriched themselves and most participated in and politely commented on each other's discoveries of alignments around the British Isles. Occasionally the members excelled themselves with lateral thinking. For example, in the fourth Portfolio, the Reverend Arthur Cross mentions the fact that in Korea the native roads twist and turn in all directions. He remarks that this is said to be due to the local belief that evil spirits can only travel in straight lines, and that some ancient Korean sites are characterised by bee-line tracks radiating from a centre, possibly laid to disperse evil spirits from a site. Alfred Watkins himself noted that perhaps this was why Christian churches were often built on the lines; in order to block the communication of malign impulses. In commenting in Portfolio 7 on a recent book review which referred to the need 'to keep out evil Chinese spirits capable of moving only in a straight line', Watkins immediately saw a relevant link.

The tenor of the correspondence moves quickly and surely into the area of death rituals and burial grounds, providing an early and often overlooked insight into the link between straight lines and rituals associated with death, a matter which I shall return to in more detail in later chapters.

Portfolio 22 is dominated by appreciations of Alfred Watkins following his death in 1935. Better than most of the heartfelt eulogies pronounced was perhaps the simple comment from K. Woods: 'How did he find time and strength for all his activities?' Just before his death, Alfred Watkins had received a long and confidential letter from Major Tyler in which his concerns about the future of the Club were set out in full. The letter was also addressed to a few key members of the club and was supposed to take stock. There is no evidence that Watkins was able to read the letter, but whether he did or not, it is very possible that he died disappointed that his discovery had not made any substantive progress in the previous 12 years. More and better ley lines had certainly been discovered – in abundance, but Watkins would not have been satisfied with proof that they simply existed; he wanted to know why they existed, and this avenue had not opened up successfully. No-one had come forward to pick up his mantle, and arguments about the discovery had taken up much of his time in the last few years.

Tyler's letter was uncompromising and direct. He suggested that the name of the Club had perhaps been a mistake, as the research was leading members away from the notion of straightness.

To change the Club's name, he said, it would be necessary to abandon the original theory of the old straight track, to clear the mind of all preconceived ideas and to try to solve the real problem behind Watkins's original theory. Club members had been finding straight tracks for years. There was little point, he said, in continuing with this activity indefinitely.

However, this contemplation occurred against a background of what appeared to be the increasingly popular phenomena of ley hunting. In the 1930s many contemporary books and mainstream articles had treated ley hunting as a justifiable, if slightly eccentric, part-time activity; even the *Church Times* ran a major feature on ley hunting which was serialised over several weeks in 1935. After Watkins's death – which was noted widely in the national press – his ideas continued to be espoused by others in the Straight Track Postal Club, and the development of the theory continued under the guidance of Major Tyler until the outbreak of the Second World War.

As a precursor to the post-war revival of ley hunting, in Portfolio 28, Major Tyler asks: 'Have we any dowsers in the Straight Track Club? Myself, I do not seem to have any capacity that way'. Dowsing had recently been popularised, and an article by Captain Boothby in the *Journal of the British Society of Dowsers* (Vol II, no. 10, pp. 115–16, 1935) suggested that natural springs could be found under every long barrow and tumulus that the author had tested, including Stonehenge and the Adam and Eve Stones in Avebury. Alfred Watkins's son, Allen, welcomed this news and predicted that dowsing 'may lead us to the veritable origin of mark points and go far to explain why these points were originally significant and sacred'.

When the War broke out, some correspondence seems to have continued between particular members of the club, but a large amount of documents were apparently lost, presumed stowed away at some point for safe-keeping. The successor to Major Tyler as Club Secretary was E.H. Carr-Gomm, who maintained what appears to have been a desultory correspondence with Allen Watkins, but almost no records survive of the period between 1939 and 1945. One of the last entries is from Carr-Gomm, who proposed a meeting of all club members in Hassocks, West Sussex. The meeting, scheduled in the week that Britain declared war on Germany, was badly attended, and it would seem that no further gatherings took place.

The Straight Track Postal Portfolio Club did not prosper after the War, petering out in 1947, but the meticulous and well-organised collection of extensive material on ley lines provides an extraordinarily rich store of research on early ley hunting and ancient sites. The surviving material is now located in the public library in Hereford.

Despite the gradual disintegration of the Straight Track Club and its members' loss of faith in Watkins's original vision, the value of Watkins's discovery should not be underestimated. He was one of the first visionaries spearheading a modern change in attitude towards our ancient heritage. Alfred Watkins was a well-respected member of society; his archaeological experience was considerable, as was his knowledge of local and natural history. The apparent aberration in his formidable CV was the ley hypothesis. This flash of insight, this revelation, came towards the end of his life and can be seen as the culmination of his life-long interest in history and the natural world. Wild claims about the hidden or lost aspects of the ancient past proliferate these days, but to make such a claim in the less blasé 1920s was to put one's head on the block. That Watkins did this without concern for his reputation displays a considerable faith in his discovery.

It is the magical and poetic qualities of the revelation that still stir the imagination as we approach the Millennium, and still prompt us to question our acceptance of the world as we see it and our place in it. Watkins inspired a new generation of ley hunters who developed an unorthodox approach to pre-history and created an 'alternative archaeology', which, while always attacked and derided by the archaeological establishment, has been the precursor of many subtle changes of attitude and approach within that establishment.

CHAPTER 3
ASTRONOMICAL ALIGNMENTS

To Alfred Watkins ley lines were only ever prehistoric trackways; even when he started to unearth leys that couldn't possibly have been tracks he continued to fit the findings to his original theory. Members of the Straight Track Club however began to realise that there was more to the profusion of landscape alignments than could be explained away by the old straight track theory.

One aspect of Watkins's alignments that has since developed into a discipline of its own is that of ancient astronomy. In *The Old Straight Track*, Watkins included a chapter entitled 'Sun Alignment' in which he argued that some ley lines may have been determined with reference to the rising sun on specific days of the year. He says: ' . . . it has become plain that the topographical sites used for sun alignment and those for the ley are in some cases identical.' A promising place to look for astronomical alignments of this type is Stonehenge, and this is where Watkins first turned his attention, having been alerted to the possibility of an astronomical connection after reading the works of the eminent astronomer Sir Norman Lockyer.

Stonehenge is probably the most famous megalithic monument in the world; its form of construction is unique, its stones the biggest of any other circle in Britain. Another celebrated feature is the approximate alignment of the centre of the circle of stones, the outlying Heel Stone and earthen Avenue with the summer solstice sunrise. Though the astronomical aspects of Stonehenge were dramatically brought to public attention in 1963 by the astronomer Professor Gerald Hawkins it had always been a tradition amongst the people of nearby Amesbury to gather at the stones before dawn on Midsummer's Day to watch the sun rise over the Heel Stone. This particular ritual was later adopted by modern druid revivalists until the public disorder and subsequent police presence at the site in the 1980s put a stop to this regular spectacle. In recent years the Druids have been allowed back to Stonehenge on the summer solstice, although the general public is still excluded.

In 1740 the antiquary William Stukeley was the first to record that the axis of Stonehenge and the Avenue leading away from it point to the north-east, 'whereabouts the sun rises when the days are longest'. He also noted, by way of an illustration, that this line was marked on the horizon by an artificial mound on Haradon Hill (see Directory: A Sunrise Line). Other antiquaries followed, notably Dr John Smith, in 1770, whose observations at Stonehenge led him to suggest that the whole area around the monument was laid out as an elaborate calendar system incorporating outlying barrows and representing a vast planetarium. In 1846 the Reverend E. Duke, in *Druidical Temples of Wiltshire*, suggested that most of the county once consisted of a huge model of the solar system based around a meridian line 32 miles long centred on Silbury Hill and that ancient monuments on circles drawn around Silbury were related to one another as planets around the sun.

By the 1890s the astronomical interpretation of ancient monuments began to take on a greater scientific aspect. Sir Norman Lockyer – astronomer, scientist, and founder and editor of the distinguished scientific journal *Nature* – began investigating the temples of ancient Egypt to test a hypothesis that they were deliberately constructed to point towards the rising and setting of the heavenly bodies at particular times of the year. He found, for example, that the temple of Amen-Ra at Karnak has its main axis directed to sunset at the summer solstice. With the knowledge that the rising and setting points of the sun in a particular location change regularly over a period of time, he attempted to date the temple by calculating how far off a true orientation the temple was in his day from what would have been the true orientation at the time the temple was constructed.

In 1901 Lockyer turned his attention to Stonehenge and attempted to date the monument by the same means. However, where Amen-Ra had an axial passageway 500 yards long giving an accurate alignment, Stonehenge was in a ruinous condition, the stones from which a true axis might have been established having been moved or disturbed. The approximate azimuth he eventually defined for the monument followed the Avenue north-east to an Ordnance Survey bench mark on Sidbury Hill. In the opposite direction the line passed over Grovely Castle hill fort six miles away and then on to Castle Ditches hill fort a further seven-and-a-half miles south-west. In 1906 Lockyer published *Stonehenge and other British Stone Monuments Astronomically Considered* which gave further evidence of geographical relationships between ancient monuments, most of which he concluded were of astronomical significance.

In 1894 Magnus Spence, an Orcadian schoolmaster, wrote an article in the *Scottish Review* outlining his observations on the remarkable group of antiquities on mainland Orkney, centred on the massive Neolithic chambered mound of Maes Howe. Other sites in the vicinity include the vast henge and stone circle of the Ring of Brodgar, the ruined henge and stone circle of the Stones of Stenness, and a scatter of tall single standing stones arranged in a pattern of alignments which can still be seen on the ground today. A principal alignment in this group of monuments runs along the passage of Maes Howe through the entrance to a single standing stone, the Barn Stone, one field away. This line points to the horizon where the midwinter sun sets. The rays of the setting sun penetrate the passage and illuminate the elaborate corbelled chamber of the mound (see Directory: Orcadian Leys). Spence claimed that additional alignments within the group of monuments pointed to other significant astronomical events. Lockyer reviewed and endorsed Spence's work, though he suggested different interpretations of his alignments.

Between writing *Early British Trackways* and *The Old Straight Track*, Watkins had read Norman Lockyer's *Stonehenge*, and this prompted him to research further the relationship between his leys and astronomical alignments. Lockyer's work showed convincingly for the first time that certain alignments through the centre of Stonehenge had been arranged to point towards the moment of sunrise or sunset on particular days of the year. Watkins lost no time in revisiting Stonehenge to follow up what Lockyer had not then fully developed – the evidence of other mark points for the alignments so described. Watkins found good evidence for four such alignments and describes these in detail in *The Old Straight Track*. One in particular has become probably the most famous ley line in England. First noted by Lockyer but not followed up (probably due to the fact that it had no astronomical significance) was the alignment of Stonehenge, Old Sarum, Salisbury Cathedral and Clearbury Ring (see Directory: Old Sarum Ley). Satisfied, Watkins summed up the results of his further research thus:

'1. That the sunrise alignments of Lockyer are identical with long distance leys;
2. That Stonehenge is at the crossing of several leys, and that it is far more probable that two of these were pre-existing and decided the site, than

that Stonehenge was the primary fact . . .
3. Several of the alignments have beacon points
on them.'

More corroboration was to come: in 1923 the journal
Archaeologia published a paper by Admiral Boyle Somerville
showing that several stone rows, circles and dolmens in the
Hebrides and Ireland have an orientation over certain stones
precisely calculated to sunrise and sunset on the quarter days
and half-quarter days. Such alignments, Somerville found,
also continued in straight lines to marks, notches, cairns or
earthworks on or near hilltops several miles away. Watkins
was evidently delighted by this discovery, and Somerville

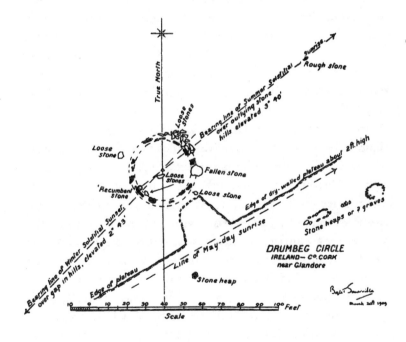

*Admiral Boyle Somerville's 1909 drawing of the
astronomical alignments through Drumbeg stone
circle, County Cork, Ireland.*

later became a trusted friend and colleague in the Straight Track Club until his death at the hands of Irish nationalists in the 1930s. Watkins, ever careful, was particularly pleased with evidence that suggested a utilitarian rather than a mystical motive: 'The material facts indicate gigantic sundials in ceremonial use. But most certainly for utilitarian – that is, season fixing – purpose.'

However, this was not the only possible explanation for these astronomical alignments and Somerville quickly concluded that other motives were at play. The Admiral was a particularly energetic and perceptive contributor to the Straight Track Club Portfolios, frequently reverting to his favourite subject of astronomy and straight tracks. One of his discoveries was the sunrise line of orientation built into the massive banked stone circle of Rannach Croim Duibh, near Lough Gur in County Limerick, Ireland. Later, the geographer and geomant Michael Dames would extend this line to include sites intimately connected with the folklore and mythology of the area (see Directory: Two Irish Leys).

In a paper entitled 'Orientation', Somerville made a perceptive observation. There was, he concluded, a forgotten connection between orientation and burial. He suggested a hilltop barrow that contained the burial of an important individual might be found to be aligned with a nearby stone circle, erected in connection with the barrow, that also aligned to a sunrise or sunset position on the horizon. He had found several examples of this practice in his researches. He suggested that it was not inconceivable that such a line of orientation might have become a trackway, firstly as a pilgrim route from the circle to the honoured grave and then later to have been extended in the same direction towards some point beyond the barrow.

This apparent connection between death and orientation (and indeed the straight line) would come to dominate later

Plate 1: The view down the passageway towards the entrance of Newgrange, Co. Meath, Ireland. The roof box can be seen above the doorway and one of the stones of the surrounding circle aligns with the passage and the midwinter sunrise.

Plate 2: The famous alignment of the centre of Stonehenge through the Heel Stone to the midsummer sunrise. Note how the top of the Heel Stone touches the horizon.

Plate 3: An artist's impression
of Alfred Watkins's discovery
of leys. A detail from the back
cover illustration to *The
Prospect Before Us* by the
Albion Dance Band.

Plate 4: (above) The Straight Track Postal Portfolio Club Summer Meeting at Hereford, July 1933. Alfred Watkins (centre) points to the mark stones and ford at Wellington, Herefordshire.

Plate 5: (left) Portrait of Alfred Watkins.

Plate 6: (above) The
funeral path between
Gotherington and
Bishop's Cleeve,
Gloucestershire. The
route, now a public
footpath, is preserved
across the cultivated
fields. The path points
towards St Michael's
Church.

Plate 7: (right) The
funeral path from
Wick to Pershore,
Worcestershire. Part of
the route across open
fields points towards
the tower of Pershore
Abbey.

ideas on the astronomical aspects of ancient sites, as well as the interpretation of many ley lines.

Watkins considered other sites beside Stonehenge in an attempt to find a common link between his leys and the rising and setting points of the sun, but it seems the lunar alignment aspects of ancient astronomy were too complex for his analysis. He described how his interest in sunrise alignments was first tested at the Giant's Cave in the Malvern Hills, Worcestershire. The cave lies at the top of the Herefordshire side of the ridge near the Herefordshire Beacon; below the cave is an unhewn boulder, a boundary stone, known traditionally as the Shew Stone or, more romantically, the Sacrificial Stone. Previous observation by others has led to the conclusion that on Midsummer's Day the sun rising over the ridge falls on the stone, and this event was interpreted as the time when the supposed 'sacrifice' used to take place. Prompted by this Watkins attempted to plot the line between the stone and the cave on the map to see if the alignment 'might have been also used as a ley'. After some investigation he found that the line passed through the Gospel Oak, Woolhope church, several sections of road, Holme Lacey church, Aconbury church and on to the highest point of Aconbury Camp. Moreover, the angle of the ley, determined by the sunrise at the stone, is reflected in the orientation of the axes of both Woolhope and Holme Lacey churches. Inspired by this discovery Watkins searched elsewhere, applying his enthusiasm for place names to other sites with possible sunrise alignments, noting Midsummer Hill, May Hill, Sun Rising Hill and so on, and applying azimuth angles for significant sunrise positions on a flat map.

The calculation of the position of sunrise (or sunset) on the horizon in a particular place is not straightforward. Enthusiastic members of the Straight Track Club would simply apply standard azimuth angles to the map in an attempt to find sites that lined up along them. The azimuth of sunrise, however, is dependent upon the latitude of the site, the elevation of the site and the elevation of the horizon. Each will affect the actual position of sunrise from any single place of observation. Furthermore, Admiral Boyle Somerville warned against long-distance astronomical alignments. The longer these are, he said, the less likely they are to be accurate. The natural curvature of the Earth and the changes in topography would throw the alignment completely off course as one travelled along the alignment, while any shift in the observer's elevation would change the position of sunrise despite the angle of the ley. The only true sunrise alignment could be seen from the primary observation point and its foresights. This complication didn't bother the more enthusiastic of Watkins's followers, who continued to suggest short- and long-distance sunrise alignments with little reference to the topography, thus exposing one of the dangers of map ley hunting.

Lockyer and his contemporaries met with stern opposition from the archaeological establishment of the day. In a similar manner to that in which Watkins and his ideas were to be shunned and dismissed 20 years later, Lockyer's ideas were resisted because they were at odds with the accepted historical view of ancient Britons. Prehistoric people were considered to be capable only of subsistence living, and certainly *in*capable of the intellectual thought processes necessary to observe, record and mark the complex movements of the sun and moon. Archaeologists were not astronomers, and their lack of understanding of those scientific principles also added to their mistrust and opposition to Lockyer and his followers. This situation was to persist (and in some ways still does, though for slightly different reasons) until the 1960s, when Stonehenge again became the battleground between archaeologists and astronomers.

When Professor Gerald Hawkins published a paper in *Nature* describing how he had calculated several significant

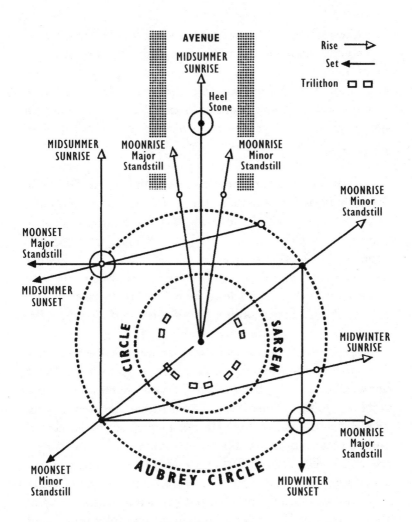

The sun and moon sightings from Stonehenge, based on an original diagram by Gerald Hawkins.

astronomical alignments between various stones at Stonehenge, it triggered a wave of popular interest in the enigmatic monument and archaeologists were forced to answer the questions posed by this remarkable discovery, questions they hoped had died with Lockyer. Hawkins's hypothesis suggests that the builders of Stonehenge had been involved in detailed observations of the heavens and that the monument was a result of these scientific investigations, recording the alignments for posterity in immovable stone. Perhaps Stonehenge was a calendrical device for fixing certain dates in the year for agricultural or religious purposes.

A few years later Hawkins's ideas were taken further by the engineer and mathematician Alexander Thom, whose meticulous surveys of stone circles and stone rows throughout Britain and Brittany led him to conclude that the megalith builders were sophisticated astronomers engaged in a detailed study of the heavenly bodies and their relative movements. These movements were incorporated into their stone monuments over a long period of observation.

Any doubt that Neolithic people were capable of observing the heavens over many years, noting the apparent regular movement of sunrises on the horizon, and constructing technically brilliant megalithic buildings in which to record such knowledge, was dispelled when the vast chambered mound of Newgrange, County Meath, Ireland was excavated in the 1960s. Traditional stories referred to the mound as *Brú na Bóinne* (Mansion of the Boyne), the home of *Mac in Dagda* (Son of the Good God), one of the *Tuatha De Danann*, a supposedly magical race of gods. Local folklore that has persisted to modern times claimed that one particular sunrise entered the chamber at Newgrange, though no-one fully understood what that meant until the excavations of the 1960s.

The excavations revealed an unusual architectural feature, a slot about a foot high immediately above the entrance to the long passageway that leads to a transepted chamber. This slot is known as the roof box and it transpires that on the morning of midwinter solstice the rays of the rising sun penetrate the centre of the mound through this precisely located slot. This feat of engineering is all the more amazing for the fact that the mound lies on sloping ground and the passage is inclined upwards. The builders had calculated the downward angle of the rays of the sun from the higher horizon on the other side of the river and positioned the roof box to align between the sun and the back of the rear chamber. In addition, one of the huge standing stones of the circle that rings the mound falls on the alignment, as does the famous decorated kerb stone immediately in front of the entrance, a stone that marks the precise alignment with a carefully defined vertical groove cut into its front face. The sun's rays do not enter the passageway directly through the entrance. On plan the passage, though not straight, follows the alignment (see Directory: Boyne Valley Leys).

Newgrange is the oldest sacred building in Europe (erected in 3300 BC), and although it may once have held cremated human remains it was almost certainly a temple and a building of great symbolic significance. It also suggests an ancient belief in the connection between death and the sun. It has been observed that Newgrange could not have been constructed as an observatory as the alignment is too inaccurate to provide any useful calendrical information. Furthermore, it seems unlikely that the spectacle of the midwinter sun illuminating an otherwise dark chamber was designed to be watched by the living. The roof box had been designed to allow the sunlight to penetrate to the centre of the mound even when the passageway was blocked off; the sun's rays were intended for the dead alone. I might even speculate here that Newgrange was designed to allow the spirits of the dead interred there to travel out and return to the mound on the rays of the sun at the instant the light penetrated the chamber. This solar (and sometimes lunar) alignment feature is common to many passage mounds in western Europe, despite variations in the construction dates and architecture of individual buildings. The connection between spirit flight and alignments will be discussed in later chapters.

Arguments about the nature of prehistoric astronomy have continued, and the scientific theories of Alexander Thom, Gerald Hawkins, John Wood, Euan McKie and others have largely been abandoned through lack of conclusive evidence in favour of a looser interpretation. The deliberate alignments built into many ancient monuments were not particularly precise. It seems that accuracy was not the prime motivation; these alignments were of more symbolic importance, and were almost certainly connected with rituals involving dead ancestors, rituals of veneration, communication and fear.

It has been observed that astronomical alignments built into a stone circle or chambered mound were sometimes enhanced by the construction of earthen banks or rows of standing stones, outlying monoliths, horizon markers such as artificial mounds (see Directory: Rhondda Cairns Ley) and notches cut into distant hills. And here we can see examples of alignments that fit the Watkins model of leys. Perhaps, as Admiral Boyle Somerville surmised, these alignments developed into processional or symbolic trackways. Not all Watkins's leys can be explained by astronomy, however. That is simply another piece of the immensely complex puzzle that is the phenomenon of ley lines.

CHAPTER 4
ANCIENT SITES AND THEIR UNUSUAL ENERGIES

The popular definition of a ley line has been unequivocal – it is a vein in the Earth along which runs a form of 'energy'. That these lines run between ancient and sacred sites throughout Britain, the standing stones, stone circles and burial mounds, seems to reinforce this notion; if the leys carry the energy, then the stones and burial chambers punctuate them and act as places of power along the network of lines. It is not difficult to understand how this idea was subsequently applied to crop circles when they began to appear with increasing regularity close to ancient sacred sites such as Stonehenge, Silbury Hill and Avebury in the late 1980s. If there is some kind of power evident at these places, then can we experience, can we see, feel and gain understanding from it?

In the 1960s society was changing rapidly; the sexual and cultural revolutions were in full swing, and mankind was riding the crest of a progressive wave. People were not only looking to the future, however, there was also a revival of interest in the past. New-found technology and achievements enabled a re-evaluation of historical culture and people looked at old stones with new eyes. 'Earth Mysteries' was coined as a catch-all phrase to describe the subject area of ancient sites and all they afford, including the craze for the UFO whose proponents had proclaimed mystical links with the old stones.

Folk memory

Mass speculation was not easy in Watkins's day, but from the 1960s mass media and communications were much more accessible and influential. Imaginative ideas about the ancient past proliferated and the belief prevailed that ancient man had been a practitioner of some sort of sacred, cosmic engineering, in touch with the Earth, and had perhaps known how to harness a natural power. Had sacred sites even enabled the ancients to communicate with other beings? If there was a latent power or energy in the Earth and our ancestors had the ability to detect and utilise it, then a memory of this might have survived in the folk mind. The examination of folklore records in this new context was beginning to yield tantalising evidence.

By far the best known studies of folk traditions in the context of Earth Mysteries studies were undertaken by the husband and wife team of photographers, Janet and Colin Bord. In their books *Mysterious Britain, The Secret Country* and *Earth Rites*, they wedded imaginative speculation to evocative photography to produce an attractive alternative view of our pre-history.

The effect of these books and others that followed was widespread. Visit the great stone circle complex at Avebury any day and you will see people laying their hands on the stones or leaning against them with their heads resting on the sarsens. Pop over to the Henge shop and buy yourself a set of dowsing rods, take them over to the stones to join the many who walk around with them, and experience that excitement and wonder when the rods twitch or cross. Many of those who have a fascination with these sites have at some time tried this for themselves and experienced a reaction from dowsing rods. But it is not only since the 1970s that people have nurtured a belief that these sites hold some kind of unexplained power or magic.

*An 18th century water diviner using the classic
forked hazel rod.*

Folklore testifies that people believed that ancient standing stones had the power to heal a variety of ailments or aid
fertility or virility. It was also widely believed that far from
being inanimate objects, the stones could come to life, and
were often fabled to walk down to streams to drink, or to
take a constitutional around the field in which they stood.
Many traditions are attached to stones which testify to their
power when correctly invoked and applied.

Until recent times the old stones have been treated with
respect and veneration by the people who live near them. In
the 19th century the villagers of Thoresby, Leicestershire,
used to hold an annual fair near the church in a field where a

large bluestone once stood, and games were played around the stone. At Durrington, Wiltshire, a fair was held at the Cross Stones on Old May Day (13 May), and villagers would dance around the stones to musical accompaniment and afterwards feast on cakes and ale. At Fortinghall, Tayside, on 31 October (the Eve of the Celtic New Year), a bonfire of furze was built on the Bronze Age barrow known as the Mound of the Dead. And on the first day of the New Year people would gather at a ten-foot monolith on North Ronaldshay in the Orkneys, where they sang and danced together.

A complex fertility tradition can be found in the frequent legends regarding mysterious cows that give endless supplies of milk. A celebrated tale is that of the White Cow of Mitchell's Fold stone circle in Shropshire. In times of famine this white cow could be found at the stone circle at the beginning and end of each day ready for milking. She allowed each person a pailful, but if anyone tried to take more it was vowed that she would never return, a threat that came true when a witch milked the cow into a sieve and consequently milked her dry. The witch was punished by being turned into what is now the tallest stone in the circle.

Many other traditions link stones with fertility and child-birth. On the Isle of Man, a well associated with a standing stone was considered capable of promoting fertility in women. A bride-to-be would fill her mouth with water from the well and walk three times around the stone at daybreak, in a sunwise direction, before swallowing the water. A large erect stone near Doagh, County Antrim in Ireland, is perforated by a small hole, and it is the local custom for marriages to be ratified by the couple clasping hands through the hole in a ceremony known as handfasting.

Certain stones were credited with the power to cure barrenness, whilst others ensured easy childbirth. Barren women at Dingwall, Ross and Cromarty, would sit upon a stone three miles away at Brahan Wood, and in Brittany, easy childbirth was believed to result from sliding down menhirs after smearing them with butter or honey.

Until the early years of this century libations were poured into man-made cup-markings and natural hollows in stones. On the island of Westray in the Orkneys, milk was poured into a hole in the centre of one of two burial mounds known as Wilkie's Knolls. Tradition held that if the locals failed to do this Wilkie would send pestilence upon the cattle. The power of standing stones, when it was invoked, was also believed to cause crops and cattle to flourish, and Respryn Cross at St Winnow in Cornwall was visited every year, and soil dug from the ground around it and thrown over the top of the stone to ensure a good crop.

People also used to resort to ancient standing stones for healing purposes, and these traditions can be found all over Britain. Rheumatic illnesses could be prevented or cured by crawling through the holed stone of the Men-an-Tol group in Cornwall. The powers of other stones could be transferred to the patient through direct physical contact. By sitting in a seat formed in Canna's Stone in Dyfed, a person could be cured of the ague; the best method was to sleep on the stone after drinking the waters of the nearby well. The Long Stone at Minchinhampton in Gloucestershire has a hole through it and it is said that children or babies used to be passed through to cure them of rickets. Probably the most well-known legend of the healing properties of ancient stones is that of the Stonehenge megaliths, as recounted by Geoffrey of Monmouth in his *History of the Kings of Britain*. In the legends he cites the stones as being 'of medicinal virtue'; by washing the stones and placing the sick in the waters their illnesses would invariably be cured. 'There is not a stone there', he wrote, 'which has not some healing virtue'.

Other traditions and stories describe standing stones that turn in their holes or move at certain times of the day or year. The Waterstone at Wrington will dance when the full moon falls on Midsummer's Day; the Nine Stones on Belstone Common, Devon, dance daily at noon; the Wimblestone, near Shipham in Dorset, was once seen dancing in the moonlight on a heap of gold; the Giant's Stone at Yetnasteen on Rousay in the Orkneys walks to a nearby loch for a drink on New Year's morning; the Wych Boulder at Wych, Lincolnshire, turns over when the clock strikes twelve; the Colwall Stone, Worcestershire, does a complete turn when the clock strikes midnight; and the Tingle Stone near Avening in Gloucestershire runs around the field when it hears the clock strike midnight. The stories are rife and can be found the length and breadth of the country.

The Devil's work

With the advent of Christianity, the stones were labelled 'pagan' and their mythology turned from being benevolent to more malign; they were put there by the Devil or they were petrified people, sinners who had disobeyed the Sabbath, turned to stone for their disobedience. Church edicts were passed in France and Spain between AD 450–110, prohibiting visits to the stones for the cure of diseases. Other stones were 'Christianised' by carving their tops into crosses, cutting crosses into their sides or by erecting crosses on top of them. In this way the Church authorities hoped to win over the people who would still resort to the traditional holy places.

Ancient stones have long been venerated, however, and even when Christianity frowned upon such worship they were often tolerated out of a grudging respect for local beliefs. Children were told that the fairies inhabited such places; they were enhanced places that offered a gateway to the fairy world. However the Church had a different version: the Devil dwelt there. Perhaps to instill a fear of the old ways the early Church began to equate the old gods with the Devil, and tales were concocted linking the Devil with the old sacred places. The Hurlers stone circles on Bodmin Moor, for example, were said to be the stony remains of men who had dared to play the traditional Cornish game of hurling on a Sunday; the stones of Tinkinswood chambered long barrows in South Glamorgan are women dancers turned to stone. Another famous tale of dancers being turned to stone is that from Stanton Drew, Somerset. This complex of megaliths consists of three circles, two Avenues and a cove, a grouping of three upright stones and a fallen capstone, all within sight of the parish church. Known traditionally as The Weddings the stones are said to be the petrified remains of a wedding party whose celebrations continued into the Sabbath. A phantom piper (no doubt a metaphor for the Devil) continued to play beyond midnight, and his playing was so hypnotic that the wedding guests were unable to stop. The circles are said to represent the dancing guests and the cove the petrified remains of the parson, bride and groom.

Layer upon layer of folklore has developed over the years and there are now reported sightings of UFOs around such places, even alien abductions. The contents of the stories are many and varied but a common strand runs through them all – a notion that some sort of unexplained energy lies within ancient stones. But has anyone ever tried to verify this? Has anyone ever managed to measure and record this power or energy scientifically?

Dowsing and strange energy effects

Oddly, very few serious attempts have been made to catalogue this phenomenon. Some dowsers have claimed the ability to detect underground forces at ancient sites such as standing stones and stone circles, and that forces are also detectable within the stones themselves. Bill Lewis, a Welsh dowser of impeccable credentials, was the first to discover dowsing effects rising and falling within standing stones which he suggested were magnetic in nature. In 1976 he was party to an unusual experiment at a huge standing stone near Crickhowell in South Wales, when, for the first time ever, an attempt was made to measure the physical effects that dowsers had claimed existed at ancient sites. John Taylor, a professor of mathematics at King's College, London, and Eduardo Balanovski, a physicist from Imperial College, utilised a gaussmeter, a device for measuring the strength of the Earth's magnetic field, to test Bill Lewis's findings. They were able to measure a definite magnetic anomaly on the stone and the whole event was captured in Francis Hitching's television documentary *Earth Magic*.

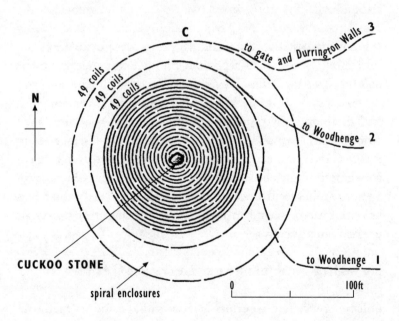

A diagram showing dowsing lines around the Cuckoo Stone, near Woodhenge, Wiltshire. The Cuckoo Stone lies on the Stonehenge Cursus alignment.

Some years later, a retired BBC engineer, Charles Brooker, enthused by the attempts of the Dragon Project to measure hidden energies at the Rollright stones did some experiments of his own. Using sensitive magnetometers Brooker found that the magnetic field intensity inside the circle of stones was significantly lower than that measured outside. Concentric bands of varying magnetic intensity inside the circle also seemed to echo the patterns that Tom Graves and others had found by dowsing.

The Dragon Project

The best attempt to investigate the belief in Earth energy at ancient sites was set up in 1976. As discussed in chapter 1, the Dragon Project was named after the traditional Chinese symbol for the Earth force or *ch'i*, and concentrated on the Rollright stones in Oxfordshire. Under the leadership of project director Paul Devereux, the aim of the Dragon Project was to detect, recognise and record this energy.

To cover all the possibilities the project took three approaches. The project's scientific co-ordinator, Dr Don Robins, took some readings at the Rollright circle using a conventional ultrasonic detector before the project commenced. These readings proved of great interest as Robins was able to conclude that there was a definite ultrasound anomaly focused on the outlying King Stone. A curious pulsing noise was detected, and even stranger was that this pulsing seemed to intensify just before and after the winter solstice, the shortest day of the year. When eventually the pulsing could be converted to an audible noise it was found that on a number of occasions the stones seemed to 'sing'. For the first time ever, tangible evidence had been found for the curious properties of the stones.

Another area of investigation was radioactivity research for which Geiger counters were used to measure variations

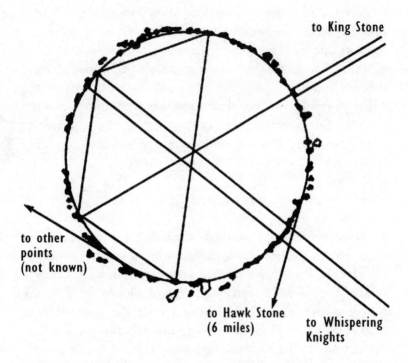

A diagram showing dowsing lines at the Rollright
Stone Circle, Oxfordshire.

in the background radiation. This background radiation is present all around us and comes from a range of sources including the Earth itself, but this should not be mistaken for 'Earth energy'. The Geiger counters were able to detect higher than normal readings within the circle, and in the road between the circle and the outlying King Stone.

The third area of monitoring was magnetism. Using sensitive magnetometers it was found that the magnetic field intensity was significantly lower inside the stone circle than outside. Further to this, significant magnetic anomalies were detected at three of the stones within the Rollright circles, more tangible evidence of unexplained energy at the stones.

Another magnetic discovery made during the Dragon Project was that certain stones at other stone circles were found to be highly magnetic. In fact, they were so magnetic that the needle of a compass could be made to turn around when held up to the stones. At Dyce stone circle in Aberdeenshire, which overlooks Aberdeen airport, the needle of a compass will turn 180 degrees when held against a certain part of the stone. Interestingly, another stone circle in Aberdeenshire, Easter Aquorthies, also has a magnetic stone and the 'hot spot' is at head height.

During its ten-year run, the Dragon Project turned its attention to other ancient sites in search of anomalies. During 1983 and 1984 the Project teamed up with the Association for the Scientific Study of Anomalous Phenomena (ASSAP) to undertake the 'Gaia Programme', one-off snapshot Geiger-counter-monitoring sessions at 30 sites all over the country. The same sessions were carried out in tandem at non-sacred locations to give a control sample. Perhaps the most interesting result of this series of monitoring sessions was the discovery of lower than normal background readings. In Cornwall, where the incidence of granite ensures higher than normal natural radioactivity, higher than normal background readings were found in the underground chambers known as fogous. This is to be expected, but at Stannon stone circle on Bodmin Moor, the local Dragon Project volunteer was unable to obtain any reading at all from the circle, despite changing the batteries in the Geiger counter. The same effect was encountered at Duloe stone circle – another radiation 'hole' in the environment. This effect was entirely reversed at the Merry Maidens, however, where the readings in the circle were considerably higher than in the surrounding environment.

All the anomalies recorded at the dozens of sites tested during the Dragon Project were in known natural energies. The only exception was the unusual light phenomenon encountered by two independent witnesses at sites that lay close to geological faults, a type of energy effect almost unrecognised by science. This effect and others like it would be investigated further by Paul Devereux in the years ahead. The effect was coined 'Earth lights' by Devereux and would eventually be proposed as a plausible explanation for many so-called UFO sightings, and remake the strange connection between ancient sites, leys and flying saucers.

The psychic angle

There was a rather less successful attempt at examining the fabled power of ancient sites in 1986. On two occasions in October of that year, a self-styled witch and neo-pagan called Kevin Carlyon organised telepathy tests at the site of the Long Man chalk hill figure on the South Downs in East Sussex. Carlyon chose the site because he believed it to be on a ley line, which for him meant 'lines of energy that are said to run across and through the land, which our prehistoric forefathers were said to be able to sense, and marked with standing stones, burial sites, hill figures etc'. It was hoped that if the Earth energy did flow through the site it would intensify the minds of those acting as 'senders' within the figure. At nine o'clock one evening the senders in the figure began psychically projecting their pictures and sounds. Other people, the 'receivers', were situated at various places around the country, but some had gone to other ancient sites including the Cerne Abbas giant and Avebury stone circle. Some people had gone to two other points on the ley line, the church and the priory in Wilmington below the Long Man, and there they waited to receive the images being sent from the people in the figure. The results were not clear-cut. Despite Kevin Carlyon's best attempts at analysis there was no startling revelation; a couple of people scored highly but the rest did not. Kevin Carlyon later went on to perform weekly rituals on the Kent coast in an attempt to stop the Channel Tunnel being built, with the same measure of success.

In 1993, paranormal investigator Andrew Collins set up Orgone 93, an attempt to recreate, or 'celebrate' as Collins would have it, some of the work of investigator Trevor James Constable, as described in his evangelistic tome, *The Cosmic Pulse of Life*. Constable was a disciple of the maverick scientist Wilhelm Reich and a believer in the existence of orgone – that strange and elusive 'life energy' that Reich claimed to have discovered and isolated back in the 1950s. Orgone, Reich believed, was a fundamental organising medium for those energies recognised by science. However, science did not recognise orgone and Reich was eventually discredited and imprisoned on tax evasion charges.

The concept of a life force is a persistent one and can be found throughout history. Each culture has its own name for it, *prana, ch'i* or *ki, wouivre*, to name but a few. Orgone was the latest in a long line of attempts to unify the various workings of nature. Reich believed that UFOs were a manifestation of the bad side of orgone, his so-called DOR, or 'deadly orgone radiation'. Constable took the UFO connection further and claimed that UFOs were constantly present in the atmosphere as orgone energy and could, under the right circumstances, be made to condense in the atmosphere and manifest themselves as UFOs. He called his ephemeral organisms 'critters'. He used psychic ritual to invoke the appearance of a critter and Constable's book is littered with photographs of blobs, smears and unrecognisable shapes superimposed upon photographs of otherwise empty, arid and featureless south-western American desert.

Inspired by Constable and the frenetic activity in the corn fields of Wiltshire during the height of the crop circle phenomenon, Collins developed a theory that crop circles were the result of the interaction of orgone energy with the environment, that there was an intelligence behind it, and that critters were regularly making their presence felt across the Marlborough Downs through the medium of strange aerial phenomena, lights in the night sky and the flattening of crops in patterns of increasing geometrical complexity. It was a short step to link these events with the proximity and profusion of megalithic and other prehistoric monuments in the area. Avebury henge, the largest stone circle in Britain, lay at the epicentre of the crop circle phenomenon, while some of the earliest crop formations had appeared in the field opposite Silbury Hill – the largest man-made mound in Europe and still not fully understood by archaeologists.

Orgone 93 set out to test the relationship between orgone energy, crop circles, earth lights, ritual landscapes and the human mind. Could Orgone 93, with similar equipment and some of the same personnel as the Dragon Project, achieve any better results? There was only one element in Orgone 93 that distinguished it from the Dragon Project and that was the co-ordinated psychic element, clearly inspired by current thinking about altered states of consciousness, ancient sites and the effects of geophysical anomalies on the brain. Sites chosen for the experiments included a hilltop site, a site near a water source, Adam's Grave, a Neolithic long barrow on the top of a hill, and a crop circle formation which appeared during the project's stay in Wiltshire. The sessions involved a period of monitoring natural radiation, electric field strength, radio frequency signals, an orgone accumulator (a device invented by Reich for trapping and storing orgone energy), and normal light and infra-red photography. The team was to attempt to create change in the environment through psychic means and by manipulation of the immediate orgone environment through the use of a cloudbuster, a device consisting of a bundle of hollow metal pipes devised originally by Reich to disperse DOR and UFOs. They hoped to measure that change by responses on the monitoring equipment, and perhaps through conscious, purposeful mental actions try to draw down some kind of anomalous energy or phenomena that could be captured on film.

Despite the great promise of this series of experiments, very little evidence of any substance was obtained. The control experiments were inadequate and rendered the few interesting anomalies that were measured virtually meaningless, while some of the photographs that were taken were later explained away as technical faults. Perhaps the most telling result was the total lack of anomalous effects measured at the crop circle site.

During the week of the Orgone 93 experiments, Doug Bower appeared at a press conference at Marlborough, a few miles down the road, in which he revealed for the first time the instruments with which he and Dave Chorley had created the first crop circles in the late 1970s, setting the ball rolling for the whole crop circle phenomenon that had resulted in Collins and his companions setting up Orgone 93. Irony indeed.

How were the sites used?

The association of magnetism and sacred sites has been noted throughout the world although, once again, little serious examination has ever been made. The ability of birds and animals to detect magnetism is well documented; in a manner of speaking, these creatures are using their own dowsing methods to navigate when migrating and returning. Humans do not have this as a recognised ability, but perhaps they once did and some may still retain it. If this is so, could this explain the magnetic patch at head height at the Easter Aquorthies stone? These magnetic stones may well have been chosen for their healing properties. Natural radioactivity is not so easy to explain, however, and human beings have no recognised ability for detecting such fluctuations.

Quite apart from the physical benefits derived from such hidden 'power', it is apparent that such sites can be places of psychic discovery as well as of healing. The sight of fairies, spirits, ghosts or even extraterrestrials at these sites has been claimed time and time again, so the mind can be affected as well as the body. Of course, this is not to suggest that everyone who visits a stone circle or burial chamber will start seeing visions, but some people do seem particularly susceptible – perhaps these are the people who have retained an ability that most of us have now lost. Similarly, some people appear to have seen and experienced ghosts, others not. It seems likely that people have variable faculties for some kind of extra-sensory perception.

In the ancient past, the tribal priest or shaman would have been one such physically gifted individual, and it was his role to commune with the spirits or the ancestors in order to gain insight and guidance. What begins to emerge here is how the concept of 'spirit' has been absorbed into the concept of 'energy' over the years. Four thousand years ago people would have visited the stones and the sacred places in the hope that their ancestors or spirits would help and guide them because that was what they knew. It is easy to see how, in a mechanised view of the world, and with current cultural assumptions, the rustic idea of 'spirit' has been replaced with the modern, hi-tech term 'energy', and that the modern version of such rituals – prayer in church – has declined considerably.

No-one is entirely sure how ancient sites were used to communicate with the spirits of dead ancestors, but the idea is widely accepted by archaeologists, and what little archaeological evidence remains does point towards elaborate rituals held at sacred sites presumably to aid the process. In particular, Neolithic chambered long barrows seem to have been a focus for ritual and ceremonial activity. It is now accepted that long barrows were not simply graves. The material evidence shows that whole skeletons were rarely interred in the chambers; the bones of the dead were brought to the long barrows long after the bodies had been allowed to decompose elsewhere. Disarticulated bones were collected and distributed amongst the chambers, while large bones such as femurs were collected together, and similarly skulls and finger bones were sorted into discrete piles. Other times they were completely jumbled up and it is almost impossible to work out how many people's remains were interred. The bones, and the skulls in particular, were removed for ritual purposes and returned afterwards; under the right state of consciousness it is possible to visualise the tribal shaman or priest communicating with the disembodied head of one of the ancestors, talking to the skull as if it was alive. It has even been suggested that certain gifted individuals had the power of the oracle and could hear voices, perhaps from the skulls of the dead, or from statues, carved heads or figurines. Today we would classify this as schizophrenia, a disability; in the past this condition may have been prized in tribal communities.

In the late 20th century we can see a growing fascination amongst Western society for the sacred places of the past; groups of largely white, wealthy Americans and Europeans spend vast sums of money visiting the ancient sites of Britain, Ireland and Brittany seeking spiritual guidance and contentment. These are sincere and intelligent people who have a deep belief in a spiritual dimension, but who have rejected traditional religion in favour of a quest for enlightenment in the power of the Earth and its traditional beliefs. The group of 20 or so people I guided around the ancient sites of the Cotswolds trooped into the cool, low chambers of a long barrow known as Hetty Pegler's Tump, near Dursley in Gloucestershire. While in the chambers they meditated and chanted and emerged feeling refreshed and recharged. They had undergone an affecting experience. If there is a power in these old places it certainly seems to be working, even today.

Ancient sites and the human mind

Nowadays, stories of alien abductions, often at ancient sites, are taken very seriously by many people. So what is behind these encounters with UFOs and creatures from other-worlds? Are they too using this 'power'?

In the 1960s the first link was made between ancient sites and UFOs. It was supposed by some that these craft from outer space were utilising the power or energy at ancient sites, and that they were even travelling along the ley lines. It is possible that a version of this somewhat far-flung propo-sition may in fact be true.

There are several known facts about the unusual proper-ties at ancient sites. There are magnetic and radioactive anomalies, on the face of it mundane and terrestrial effects. However, exposure to these two hidden powers or energies can have an odd effect on the minds of some people. In the human brain there is a small cone-shaped gland called the pineal gland. It has been suggested that this gland, when exposed to changes in the Earth's magnetic field, can cause shifts in consciousness and time-slips. Similarly, when the brain is exposed to strong electromagnetic fields, a form of epileptic attack can be triggered and various symptoms can be experienced including hallucinations, seeing odd lights, a feeling of being watched and of paralysis. The person who undergoes these bizarre 'attacks' can be completely con-vinced that the events were entirely real and physical. This may well account for some of the UFO visitation and abduc-tion stories.

The Dragon Project at the Rollright stones went on for ten years. As a footnote to some of the findings it was decided that it might prove fruitful to set up some further experiments into just how the unconscious mind is affected by the anomalous effects found at ancient sites. Anthropological and folklore evidence suggests that sleeping at particular locations could lead to altered states of consciousness, of which the dreaming state is but one. To give a few examples: the story of Jacob and his vision of a ladder reaching from earth to heaven is well known; the fact that he used a rock as a pillow cannot be mere coincidence. Similarly, legend has it that St Brynach would spend many nights sleeping on the peak of Carn Ingli in the Preseli mountains in Pembrokeshire, during which he would experience visions in which he communed with angels. Carn Ingli is so magnetic that compass needles reverse on its summit. On the top of a small hill at Lydney in Gloucestershire lie the remains of a Romano-British dream incubation temple. Situated above huge iron ore deposits and underground water sat a series of sleeping chambers; visitors would drink copiously from the spring before sleeping and dreaming in one of the cells. In the morning a therapeute would listen to them recounting their previous night's dreams and make predictions based upon them.

If the magnetic and radioactive energy can affect our brains and cause altered states of consciousness, then tests during sleep might be appropriate. Volunteers for the Dreamwork Programme slept out at various sites including Carn Ingli peak in Pembrokeshire, Carn Euny fogou underground passage, Chun Quoit dolmen and Madron Holy Well, all in Cornwall. The volunteers slept with a companion who would wait for signs of rapid eye movement in the sleeper and then wake them and ask for a detailed account of the dream. This would continue throughout the night and each session would be recorded. The object of the experiments was to see if there were any recurring themes or images that were specific to these sites. The project ran for two years from 1994 to 1996, and when all the data was collected it was sent to be analysed by Dr Stanley Krippner, a leading

investigator into dreaming and altered states of consciousness, at the Saybrook Institute in the USA. The results are
not yet available.

The past 20 years have seen thorough investigations into
the question of mysterious energies at ancient sites, so what
exactly has been discovered? The findings of the Dragon
Project show that there are definite anomalies at certain
ancient sites – fluctuations in background radiation and in
the magnetic field. The ultrasound tests carried out at
Rollright also show that something unusual happens around
the shortest day of the year, while the folklore record has
documented archaic beliefs in healing properties at the sites
and a belief that beings from other worlds could be encountered there. The findings of the Dragon Project correspond
with much that has been claimed about ancient sites, from
the detecting of energy effects to the cure of ailments and
encounters with the unearthly. However, what the Dragon
Project did not find was evidence to support the idea that
there is some unrecognised or 'cosmic' energy present at
these sites. As a consequence of this some of the theories that
had abounded about the ability to dowse ley lines of energy
at ancient sites have had to be withdrawn for sheer lack of
evidence.

The old sites *are* places of power; their magical quality
still attracts people who grapple with all the questions that
they pose. Many people visit these incredible places with preconceived ideas about cosmic forces, challenging them with
dowsing rods at dawn. But people – whether ley hunters or
not – do not have to detect unexplained energy with dowsing rods in order to experience the sites fully. All they need
are their eyes and ears; slowly and surely the stones will give
up their secrets to those determined to know them.

CHAPTER 5
RIGHT ON, STRAIGHT ON:
The importance and meaning of the straight line

The initial premise of ley lines – that they are the remnants of prehistoric trackways – is often lost in the modern quest for a meaning behind straight lines in the landscape. As every generation is supposed to get the Stonehenge it deserves or desires, so it is with the ley line. Watkins's old straight track was dismissed by the academic world of his day as nonsense. The same arguments have persisted to the present day, and although it is easy to find flaws in Watkins's claims, there are good reasons for thinking that he wasn't entirely wrong in his assertions, however it wasn't until 40 years after his death that new evidence from around the world appeared to underpin his fundamental idea. In this chapter we examine the evidence for the old straight track and come across examples of straight routes connected with the culture, ritual and religion of the living which lead us inevitably towards the uncovering of the straight tracks of gods, spirits and the dead.

Alfred Watkins was a businessman. He set up a factory to manufacture his famous 'Bee' photographic light meters. He spent a great deal of his working life travelling and he knew all the roads, tracks, paths, short-cuts and long hauls around Hereford. It is no surprise, therefore, that when asked to explain the reason behind the system of ley lines, he initially interpreted them as trader's routes. Why else, he reasoned, would prehistoric people construct straight trackways for miles across country if it wasn't for some practical purpose, namely for trade and commerce? After all, by the 1920s it was known that axe factories and flint mines had existed in Stone Age times and that prehistoric people had traded carved stone axes, flints and pottery between distant parts of the country.

In such times there was plenty of travel but no roads, so Watkins assumed that Neolithic commercial travellers must have used prominent sighting points such as hills and mountains as a means of getting around. They would make a beeline for a large or unusually shaped hill that they knew from experience was in the general direction they wanted to take. At the top of the hill other sighting points corresponding to the direction needed would then become clear. On route they might perhaps leave a small stone at a high place or a ford across a river, much as climbers do today. After many years these collections of stones could have grown into fair-sized heaps and become familiar waymarkers. In later years larger mounds of earth and stone which could be seen from a distance would have been set up along the route and taller stones put up to mark the way properly. Alternatively, notches would have been carved into the ridges of hills by the passage of many pairs of feet treading the pathways up and over hills.

The members of the Straight Track Club often unearthed references to straight tracks from other parts of the world in an attempt to provide corroborative evidence for Watkins's ideas. One particularly attractive reference can be found in Portfolio 14, where W.H. McKaig refers to a letter published in *The Observer* on 5 January 1930. The writer had described how she had lived for many years in Ceylon and that the 'aborigines' had to travel long distances to the salt pans. She noted that their tracks always ran perfectly straight through the forest, were sighted on some distant hill and that the way was marked at intervals by large stones similar to those found marking old tracks in Britain. The sighting hill was referred to as a 'salt hill' and the mark stones as 'salt stones' and she remarked on the similarity to Watkins's salt tracks.

The green roads of England

Was Watkins right about the ley line as a trade route? After all, such roads don't have to be straight. Admittedly, the quickest route between two places is a straight line 'as the crow flies', and this might seem the obvious route to take, but steep hills, deep and fast flowing rivers, cliffs and boggy lowlands would all have presented great difficulties to the trader, laden with goods or encumbered by cattle. Britain's oldest known road, the prehistoric Ridgeway,is not particularly straight. As its name implies, it follows the ridges of hills as it snakes its way from the Thames at Streatley in Berkshire to the Wiltshire Downs and beyond. The Ridgeway follows the high ground for very sensible reasons. It would usually be dry in winter (unlike the marshy valleys) and its height above the surrounding country side would give the traveller a good view of where he was going and how far he had come, as well as providing improved security against unexpected attacks. The Ridgeway is but one of a network of ancient trackways that once connected the whole of the country; none of them are dead straight.

Other later roads were not straight either, for example the old drove roads which were used to transport livestock from one side of the country to the other. In nature, animals do not tend to take the straight path, and many early tracks would certainly have evolved from animal tracks at a time when hunting provided the primary source of food. The green roads of England were also seldom straight, following as they did the natural contours of the landscape. People either walked or rode on horseback so roads did not have to be wide, and the matter of straightness or steepness was of little importance. Steep gradients and boggy ground would naturally be avoided, but much travel would have been in a straight line on the level and when it was dry underfoot. The winding road was probably the result of the introduction of wheeled vehicles in historic times.

Watkins was well aware of the old ridgeways and green roads of England and he later modified his theory to account for the wandering nature of ancient roads. He approved of G.K. Chesterton's famous verse about the 'reeling road'. Although the track may have meandered and diverted to cross rivers and to avoid steep inclines, he said, the mark points along the route would be laid out in a straight line so that the track would always return from its wandering course to the next point along the line.

Despite some initially half-hearted attempts to come to terms with Watkins's discovery, the archaeologists of the day were highly sceptical. But some of the scepticism was understandable: unless all of Watkins's leys were the product of coincidence, what did they actually mean? Watkins and his immediate followers had a great deal of enthusiasm for drawing straight lines on the map, but this sort of activity would lead nowhere without getting out and walking the lines in the field. If Watkins was right, and leys were trackways, then it should be possible to see one mark point from the other and be able to make one's way along the original route. If this is not possible then, at best, some of the mark points had been lost or destroyed; at worst, the line was simply a product of chance.

Roman roads

Straight roads didn't officially appear in Britain until the Roman invasion, and Watkins's discovery of leys was originally prompted by his attempts to trace the lost courses of the Roman roads around Hereford. He believed that the Romans had, in many cases, simply adopted existing ancient British trackways and built their new roads over them without the need for further surveying. It is true that some Roman roads are aligned on ancient pre-Roman monuments, and one such example can be seen near Avebury in Wiltshire where a preserved section of Roman road in a field next to the modern Devizes to Swindon road can be seen to point directly towards Silbury Hill, the largest man-made mound in Europe. Another is the Fosse Way, which aligns directly upon the prominent Bronze Age mound at Brinklow in Leicestershire. Even more curious are Roman roads which appear to point directly towards church towers and spires built centuries after the Romans left Britain. A prime example of this can be found in Cirencester in Gloucestershire, where the course of Ermine Street (now a modern road) heads directly towards the massive tower of Cirencester church.

There were practical reasons for the Romans to build straight roads: they had to move armies and supplies around the country quickly and by the most direct route. But it is not inconceivable that the first roads built during the conquest of Britain were engineered over the courses of existing trackways and roads. Excavations beneath Watling Street, Ermine Street and the Fosse Way have revealed the paving stones of earlier roads. It is also known that the indigenous Britons had the chariot; such vehicles would be ineffective if decent roads had not been available to run them on. The Icknield Way and Peddar's Way are other examples of older trackways Romanised by the invaders.

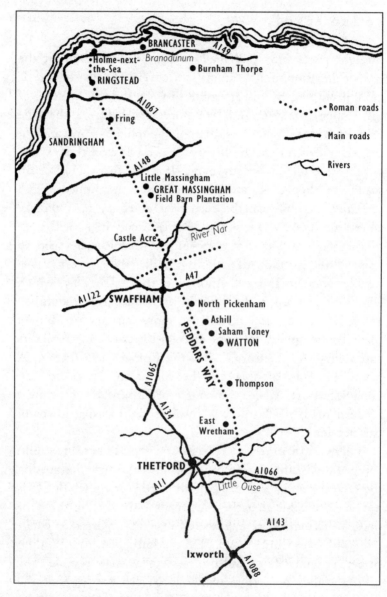

Peddar's Way, Norfolk. A remarkably straight Roman road.

Like Watkins's prehistoric ley men, the Romans had to deal with natural obstructions such as hills and rivers, and the routes of Roman roads up hillsides can be seen to deviate from a straight line until they reach the summit before resuming the straight course of the road. All over the south of France, a Roman occupied area, towns and villages are at the tops of hills, with a snaking road curling to the summit, but often with a straight road at the foot of the hill. Elsewhere, the straight course of the road, sighted on a prominent hill or geographical feature when forced to deviate, was quickly brought back on course, often with severe changes of direction. The construction of the Roman road network in Britain was a large-scale planning exercise and the existence of parallel stretches of road, and roads at right angles to each other, testify to the skills of the Roman surveyors. Probably the best example of Roman road alignment is the Fosse Way, which runs from Exeter to Lincoln and which originally linked together a series of forts set equidistant along the route. The alignment is 200 miles long and deviates only eight miles over its whole length in order to avoid difficult terrain. The longest straight section of Roman road in Britain is on the Peddar's Way in East Anglia, a length of 22 miles.

Apart from the need to get from point A to point B quickly, the other reason for straightness may well have been the symbolism of power. Nothing is likely to demonstrate your complete superiority more than being able to take the straight and direct route through a conquered country. The straight road showed you were in control, of both the landscape and its people. It is this link between straightness and imperial power, government and kingship, that may offer further clues to the understanding of the straight landscape line.

Kingship and morality

Like Watkins we can find words in our language that hint at
the link between imperial power and straightness. Modern
English is the result of many centuries of evolution and contains fragments of many other older languages. One of the
oldest is Indo-European, which can still be found in many
European languages. The Indo-European root-words *reg* and
rect mean 'movement in a straight line' and can be found in
modern words such as regular, rectangle, direction, region
and so on. The same root words also surface in other modern words which are associated with moral behaviour, kingship and order, such as right, righteous and rectitude, regal,
regency, reign, royal and ruler. The word 'ruler' is a good
example of the crossover in meaning, conveying the concept
of imposing moral and political authority on subjects as
well as determining and maintaining the boundaries of a
kingdom.

The Romans were well practised in the laying out of land
into an ordered system, and the principle of 'centuration' is
well established. From a central point, the 'umbilicus' or
navel, straight roads were laid out in the four cardinal directions, a sacred stone marking the centre. The Romans built
rectilinear street patterns in their towns and a system of radiating roads, which symbolised their imposition of order upon
the countries they conquered. This principle of ordering the
landscape was a tool of imperial power that can be found in
similar forms elsewhere in the civilised world. The ancient
emperors of China, for instance, built their Forbidden City
complex in Peking, at the heart of the Empire, on a rectilinear grid from which royal roads ran to the four cardinal
points. In this way the divine influence of the Emperor could
spread out into the four quarters of the land.

The association of straight roads and imposed order survived into recent centuries. The great parks of England were

laid out with radiating straight roads like the spokes of a wheel leading out from the great house. The Mall in London is a classic example of the straight royal road leading to (or from) Buckingham Palace which is still in use today. Even in modern times we are still building deliberately straight lines into our towns. At the centre of the new town of Milton Keynes the three main boulevards are laid out in parallel straight lines pointing in the direction of the midsummer sunrise, but this was a purely fanciful piece of design and isolated within a wobbly grid of modern roads designed to inhibit the speed of modern vehicles. The Milton Keynes boulevards are a hollow reminder of a principle once held to be of great importance.

A curious example of a link between straightness and kingship can be found in the portfolios of the Straight Track Club of 1927. W.H. Fox mentions a story relating to the Manor Gotham in Nottinghamshire. King John and his followers, on their way from Nottingham, decided to take a short cut at Cuckoo Bush near the village of Gotham in order to follow a straight track across the meadows. The villagers of Gotham tried all manner of ways to prevent this as they believed that wherever the King passed through, the royal track became a public pathway forever; such was the power of the King and the law.

The link between imperial power and straightness goes back a long way. The Kilmartin valley in Argyllshire in Scotland is the location of a great number of prehistoric monuments; stone circles, standing stones and chambered cairns litter the valley floor. In this valley lies a classic ley line: a dead straight alignment of huge chambered burial mounds (see Directory: A Scottish Royal Ley). This is an accepted deliberate alignment of tombs of ancient kings. Unnoticed or unmentioned in the academic literature is the fact that the line through the tombs, when extended, passes through three forts, one of which sits on top of a conical hill. This line is clearly not a trader's trackway. It is a symbolic line linking the burial places of kings with their seats of power (the forts) and a prominent hill. This line is a symbol of kingship as powerful as any Imperial Roman road.

The second link with straightness, which also relates to divine kingship, is moral authority. In his search for historical references to the old straight track, Watkins found several in the Bible linking the straight path and the ways of righteousness. For example:

'I will go before thee, and make the crooked places straight' Isaiah 45:2

'Make straight paths for your feet' Hebrews 12:13

'For at the first she will walk with him by crooked ways, and bring fear and dread upon him, and torment him with her discipline until she may trust his soul and try him by her laws. Then she will return the straight way unto him and comfort him, and shew him her secrets' Ecclesiasticus 4:17

'Prepare ye the way of the Lord, make his paths straight. Every valley shall be filled, and every mountain and hill shall be brought low; and the crooked shall be made straight, and the rough places shall be made smooth' Luke 3:4

'Make thy way straight before my face' Psalms 5:8

'Their thoughts are thoughts of iniquity;
Wasting and destruction are in their paths,
The way of peace they know not;
And there is no judgement in their goings:
They have made them crooked paths' Isaiah 59:7

'I will cause them to walk unto the river of
waters in a straight line wherein they shall not
stumble' Jeremiah 31:9

The association of moral rectitude with the 'straight and narrow' path can be seen clearly in Bunyan's *Pilgrim's Progress*,
an allegorical tale of a pilgrim's journey through life and the
moral dilemmas he faces on the way to salvation. The story
takes the form of a journey across country along a straight
track, a symbol Bunyan obviously borrowed from the Bible.
On route Bunyan's Pilgrim, Christian, is beset by distract-
ing companions. He is directed by Good-Will:

'Look before thee; dost thou see the narrow way?
That is the way thou must go; it was cast up by
the patriarchs, the prophets, Christ, and his apostles; and it is as straight as a rule can make it. . .
But thus thou may'st distinguish the right from
the wrong, the right only being straight and narrow.'

Pilgrim's Progress, Watkins maintains, is nothing less than a
folk memory of the old straight track in England. From the
start point, the pond, the causeway through it, the wicket
gate and the beacon light beyond, are all made by Bunyan
to be sighted in one straight line.

Pathways to the gods

However insistent Watkins may have been that his alignments were the remnants of a system of old straight tracks,
the direct evidence for this was sparse. It is true that he found
many straight fragments of roads and tracks aligning with
his mark points; in their survey of English leys in the late
1970s Devereux and Thompson also found numerous exam-

ples of ancient tracks falling on map leys. But without veri-
fication of the age of those tracks the coincidence of map
alignment and straight track could only be one of surmise,
however tantalising. So, at a time when the straight track
explanation for leys was beginning to lose favour with post-
war ley hunters, along came a book that caused great excitement and provided a desperately needed boost for serious ley
researchers.

In 1978 Tony Morrison's book *Pathways to the Gods* was
published. In it was a remarkable collection of aerial photographs, which appeared to show dead straight tracks running
for miles across the deserts and pampas of South America.
It seemed that Morrison had rediscovered a Watkinsian ley
system intact half-way across the globe. Morrison, a zoolo-
gist by training and a filmmaker by profession, had developed an interest in the enigmatic desert markings at Nazca
in Peru. These straight lines, geometric shapes and zoomor-
phic images had received notoriety in the 1960s when the
Swiss writer Erich von Däniken, in a well-publicised and
serialised book, claimed that they were the landing strips of
extraterrestrial spaceships.

The Nazca lines have been studied for many years and it
still remains a mystery as to exactly why they were laid out
on the vast mountain plateau. Some of the lines connected
burial places, some were associated with ancestor cults, and
others were believed to be the routes of spirits. More
recently, anthropologists and archaeologists have linked
some of the Nazca markings with ancient rituals connected
with ensuring a regular supply of water. Large trapezoidal
markings point towards hill and mountain sources of water
and are associated with sacred sites. To confuse the matter
even further the desert plain is also home to other vast figures that overlay the lines. The plain is peppered with animal images including a monkey, a spider, a killer whale, a
hummingbird and a condor. There are also a giant hand,

flowers and a spiral, all created like the lines, by removing dark soil from the surface to expose the lighter soils beneath, which over the centuries has turned a purplish-brown colour. While some of the animal figures resembled those found on Nazca pottery, others were thought to represent mythological spirits or even visions seen by the Nazca people.

At the time Morrison first visited the Nazca lines, he met Maria Reiche, a German mathematician who had been studying the lines for 17 years. She sought proof that the vast lines led directly to the rising and setting points of celestial bodies on the horizon. As early as 1941 a history professor at Long Island University in the USA had witnessed the midwinter

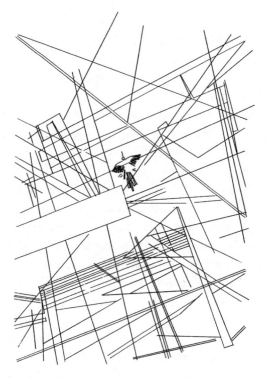

Part of the vast complex of straight pathways on the Nazca plain. The bird effigy, a condor, has a wingspan of over 350 feet.

sun setting at the end of one of the lines, which led him to describe the Nazca desert as 'the largest astronomy book in the world'. In 1968 Morrison visited Nazca again during the making of a documentary film for the BBC, where he met up with Professor Gerald Hawkins, the man who had 'cracked' the riddle of Stonehenge a few years previously. Hawkins was in the desert to test for himself the astronomical theories put forward to explain the Nazca lines. Hawkins's meticulous surveys showed that the lines deviated from a straight course by less than four yards in a mile! He made an accurate plan of the lines on the pampa, but after running a computer check on the alignments he found no significant correlation between them and positions of any stars as they would have appeared at the time the lines were believed to have been built and used.

Documentary records from 1586 refer to an ancient people who lived at Nazca before the Incas, and had built roads, still visible then, as wide as a street. It is possible that Nazca lines were used as roads, although their profusion makes this doubtful. There doesn't seem to be any astronomical explanation either. So what were the lines built for?

It wasn't until 1977 that Morrison returned to South America in search of an explanation for the old straight South American track. Apparently unaware of Watkins or leys, Morrison's discoveries and observations seem all the more important as he uncovered a system of ancient straight trackways, still in existence and still being used by local people, all of which conformed almost exactly to the original Watkins model.

Morrison was directed to a place 25 miles north of the Nazca pampa where other dead straight lines had been found in the desert. He found a line a mile long pointing directly to a large hill. At the other end was a low mound. Unlike the Nazca lines this line had been made from small heaps of stone set approximately two yards apart with a smooth path running to one side. Large stone heaps had been placed at both ends of the line. In the same area he found other lines and large cleared areas similar to those found at Nazca. In many cases Morrison found that the lines connected one centre with another, often a site in the valley to another on the higher pampa. A small number simply ended in the desert as a deliberately placed heap of stones.

At Collique, near Lima, Morrison was shown a place where lines radiated form a central hub like the spokes of a wheel, but they were clearly not highways. Straightness, however, was a common feature with all the examples he found. The answer to this enigma he was told was 'beyond mathematics' and would be found in the Andean mind, in the customs and religion of the people who built the lines. At the site of Collique, American anthropologists had discovered coca leaves placed deliberately under a stone. The Indians would leave coca, a traditionally used and respected stimulant, as an offering to their gods and spirit places. These spirit places were called *wak'as* and included stones, hills, springs, caves and other inanimate objects – even the mummies of ancestors. Many seemed to be connected in some way by straight lines or tracks.

The old straight South American track

At Cuzco in Peru, Morrison stumbled across a possible explanation. In his book, *The History of the New World* (1653), Jesuit Father Bernabè Cobo referred to *ceques* (pronounced 'seek'is') in the ancient Inca city of Cuzco. These were lines on which *wak'as* were placed and which were venerated by the local people. *Ceques* had been described as sacred pathways, while some regarded them as boundaries or lines of stones, the old Indian word *ceqque* or *ceque* means 'boundary' or 'line'.

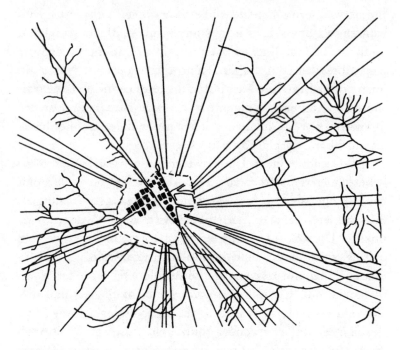

Ceques, *invisible straight lines linking shrine sites, radiating out from the ancient Peruvian city of Cuzco.*

Cobo described how *ceques* radiated outwards from the Temple of the Sun at the centre of the old Inca capital, but these lines are not the same as the lines at Nazca. For a start they are not visible, being only apparent in the alignments of *wak'as* (in much the same way Watkins's leys are invisible), which has led modern archaeologists and historians to refer to *ceques* as 'invisible lines', or 'arbitrary', 'imaginary' or even 'lines of force'. If the *ceques* had originally been paths why was there no trace of them now? Perhaps they had grown over and been lost in the intervening centuries, or perhaps, as 17th century edicts of the Roman Catholic Church had instructed, the holy shrines along the routes of the *ceques* had been destroyed. Perhaps

the natives destroyed the paths themselves in order to prevent the Spanish from locating their holy places. We don't
know. As in Europe during the spread of early Christianity,
pagan holy places around Cuzco were destroyed and built
over with churches and Christian shrines. Morrison was
shown one remarkable alignment, which may have been on
a *ceque*, of five churches and a shrine crossing the city from
east to west.

The *ceques*, it seems, were arranged to radiate outwards
from the Temple of the Sun between two lines at right
angles, which divided the city into four and extended out
into the Inca Empire. Although the form of the *ceques* was
unknown, each was in the care of a particular family and
wak'as were placed on the lines like holy stopping places.
These *wak'as* mostly took the form of stones, springs, hills,
or stones on hills, and others were open places, like the
cleared areas of squares at Nazca. Offerings were made at
the *wak'as*, often in the form of human sacrifices, usually of
small children. These *Qhapaq Hucha* ceremonies began in
Cuzco and culminated in a sacrifice at specially designated
sites (*wak'as*), often located near the summits of holy mountains. The sacrifices were an annual event but were also
invoked at times of great disaster. Documentary records
made by the Spanish invaders record that the *Qhapaq Hucha*
children were brought to Cuzco in solemn procession along
the Inca roads and then taken to their chosen place of
sacrifice along *imaginary straight lines* that began at Cuzco
and stretched to the ends of the Empire.

Despite his attempts to track down sufficient proof that
the *wak'as* did indeed lie on straight lines, the profusion of
sites made it impossible to confirm Morrison's suspicions.
His Andean ley hunt had drawn a blank. A possible answer
lay further south in the *altiplano* of Bolivia. His search led
him to the Bolivian capital of La Paz where an examination
of aerial photographs taken by the cartographers of the

Military Geographic Institute revealed a confusing network of lines near the Bolivian border with Chile. There were also isolated long straight lines, sets of parallel lines and the same radiating spoke patterns as he had found at Nazca, but unlike the Nazca pampa there were no cleared areas nor were there any animal figures.

The terminal points of the lines comprised mostly of hills and rocky places, but many were marked by white-painted *capillas* or chapels built at the ends of the lines or on the tops of the hills. These *capillas* are still venerated by modern-day Indians. French anthropologists in the 1920s had recorded these paths converging at the hills on which were perched these small shrines, but were unable to determine what they were for.

Morrison decided to try to photograph some of the lines on the *altiplano* from the air in the region of the Sajama volcano. He found lines leading in all directions running unerringly straight over hills and gullies (see Plate 9). Some of the lines were still in use as paths, some led to small, white-painted *capillas* standing on hilltops, others to open scrubland, petering out to nothing. One line in particular ran for 30 kilometres, dead straight with no regard to the terrain. At one point it disappeared under extensive sand dunes only to reappear on the other side.

Later investigations on the ground revealed that some of the lines had been kept clear of vegetation in recent times and that offerings of symbolic broken pottery, called *jik'illta*, used as money in religious festivals, had been laid on the lines. Other lines had clearly been abandoned and were being lost to the scrub. These were lines in profusion, with hills and stones being the most frequently found terminal points. As described, the hills were usually crowned with white *capillas*, often topped with a cross, which could have been built at any time since the arrival of the Spanish, or may have been earlier shrines that were

Christianised by the invading missionaries. For the ancient Aymara Indians, the hilltops were once sacred places, occupied by undefined spirits. According to local tradition, the highest hills were the most venerated and if the paths led over lower hills to reach the higher ones the way was marked by intermediate shrines. The parallels with Watkins's leys are again apparent.

The *wak'as* along the paths varied in size and form, but were often small piles of stones. Some *wak'as* were designated as places of contemplation, others were built to mark places where unusual events had occurred. The landscape, in the Aymaran mind, was populated by dozens of spirits who controlled the workings of nature. Local villagers told Morrison that the paths were always dead straight where they were connected with holy places, while other paths could wander where the course was easier. The straight paths ran directly over hilltops and climbed at impossibly steep gradients.

Everything points to a simple, if vague, religious use of the lines. Although some can be shown to have a loose astronomical or calendrical use, Morrison was forced to conclude that the *wak'as* or natural mark points on the lines were linked with modern religion or ancient Earth spirits. At Nazca the lines may well have been constructed for ancestor worship with the *wak'as* representing the spirits of ancestors. In remote Andean villages straight paths climb the local holy hill where the villagers believe the spirits of their ancestors dwell see (Plate 10). On holy days after dancing in the village square the Aymara Indians go in procession along the straight paths, making offerings along the way, to the shrines perched on the hill at the end of the lines.

Morrison was fortunate to have stumbled across the Andean lines when he did, for although some of the sacred pathways and their shrines were still in use then, many had been abandoned. The younger generations no longer hold the ancient beliefs of their parents and grandparents and the whole system is beginning to fall into disrepair. Eventually the lines will fade, leaving only the piles of stones for future investigators to puzzle over.

Only in America . . .

Elsewhere in the Americas fragments of straight road systems can still be traced. Whether all these various straight roads or paths have a common purpose is not clear, but a unifying factor is that they invariably link holy or sacred places. In Portfolio 14 of the Straight Track Club Watkins remarked:

> 'I might as well refer here to a similar layout in Yucatan, South America, described by Dr Ganns, *Ancient Cities and Modern Tribes* (Duckworth, 1926). He found running through the jungle, a great causeway, 32ft wide, elevated from 2–8ft above the ground, constructed of large blocks of stone. It ran as far as we followed it straight as an arrow, and almost as flat as a rule. The guide told us that it extended for 50 miles direct to Chichen-Itza (it started from the other chief named town of Coba) and that it ended at the great mound, 2km to the north of Nohku or main temple in a great ruined building.'

This example of the Mayan *sacbe* is the longest of 16 known roads which originate in Coba, Mexico. Whilst it can be argued that the *sacbeob* (plural) were used as physical roads, others have suggested that they were conceptual lines of communication of a religious and social nature that were, occasionally, marked out as stone causeways. This might explain why a complete system has never been found.

Since the advent of infra-red satellite photography, straight ritual roads have been discovered in New Mexico in the United States. These roads are barely visible at ground level and run straight out from Chaco Canyon, the site of many ancient ruined ceremonial and religious buildings, known as *kivas*. The roads were made by clearing the surface of small stones and placing them alongside the line of the track. As in Bolivia, some of these roads run parallel to one another and others go nowhere, petering out in the desert. This suggests that the primary use of these roads was not for simple trade or transportation. The ancient Anasazi Indians who made the roads did not have wheeled vehicles or horses. Detailed study of the road patterns from satellite photographs reveal that, rather than linking communities, they connect specific places in the landscape, suggesting a symbolic rather than practical purpose.

One of the major sites connected with the Anasazi roads is Pueblo Alto. Extensive finds of broken pottery around the site suggest religious activity of some kind. Many roads converge on the *kiva*, and broken pottery has also been found at places along the roads. The breaking of pottery is regarded as a votive offering all over the world, and like the pottery fragments found on the Bolivian lines, these remains may well have had a similar symbolic function, linking the straight roads and the stopping places along it with Earth spirits and the spirits of ancestors.

The fairy paths of Ireland

It has been suggested that the *ceques* of Cuzco may have been conceptual lines rather than physical paths, whose courses can only now be traced by the shrines still remaining on the lines. A remarkably similar type of conceptual line can be found on the other side of the Atlantic in Ireland. W.Y. Evans-Wentz travelled extensively in the 'Celtic' parts of Britain and France earlier this century collecting fairy stories, which later appeared in his book, *The Fairy Faith in Celtic Countries*. He wrote about the fairy paths in Ireland, sometimes visible as old roads, but frequently only preserved in folk memory. The fairy paths or passes are invisible, mythical routes used by the fairies or the 'little people' on their seasonal journeys between their dwelling places. Fairy dwelling places include small hills and hillocks, often the sites of *raths*, circular defensive earthwork enclosures of known antiquity. *Raths* were known to local people as fairy forts. Anyone unlucky enough to be standing on a fairy pass when the fairies moved through the land was likely to be struck dead or carried off. It was the custom for those whose house was built across a fairy pass to leave the front and back doors open when the fairies were on the move so as to allow them free passage.

In the 1950s Diarmuid MacManus recounted a number of tales from living memory about the dangers of obstructing the fairy path, which suggest that the passes were straight. A certain Mickey Langan had decided to build himself a new house but took the precaution of checking on the location of nearby fairy forts so that he could select a site that did not lie on a direct line between them. That way he would be assured that his new house would not hinder the movement of the fairies. Another fellow, Paddy Baine, had built a house without consultation with the local seer and after taking up residence was plagued by disturbances which threatened to shake the house down to the ground. He had built up against the side of a lane. The local wise woman advised him to remove the corner that abutted the road as it was impeding the progress of the 'good people'. The local stonemason sliced off the offending corner and the disturbances subsequently ceased. Finally, Michael O'Hagan lost his eldest son through a mystery illness that baffled the local doctor. His second son then fell ill and died. Still the mystery illness could not be identified. Eventually four more children died and still the malady continued to affect his remaining children. Eventually, recourse to the local wise woman revealed the somewhat unusual reason for the problem. Six months before his troubles began O'Hagan had extended his cottage west (a practice frowned upon by traditional wisdom), into an open field (even worse) and (most dangerously) into a *straight line between two fairy forts* (my italics). A night's work with a pickaxe saw the extension demolished and the surviving children rapidly recovered.

Little work has been done on trying to identify the geographical location of fairy passes in Ireland, and it has been argued without any real hard evidence that they are not necessarily straight. Certainly, preliminary map work has revealed that *raths*, which are plentiful in parts of rural Ireland, can frequently be found to align with each other and with natural mounds in true Watkinsian fashion. A query in Portfolio 20 of the Straight Track Club mentions the discovery by Dr Graves, the Bishop of Limerick and fellow of Trinity College, Dublin, of a principle in the arrangement of *raths*, which was believed to lead to important results in establishing the ancient geography of Ireland. He had made a connection between the alignments of three cup marks on ancient stones and the frequent alignment of *raths* in groups of three on the ordnance maps and surmised that the cup mark stones were diagrams of the *raths* in the district.

Gordon McLellan, writing in *The Ley Hunter*, reported his investigation of a straight road leading from a fairy mound at Streedagh, aligning to two further fairy forts and the fairy mountain of Benbulbin – an unusually flat-topped mountain in County Sligo. He also discovered an unmetalled track running due west from a fairy fort south of Streedagh, past an unnamed mound and eastwards through two groups of fairy forts and on to the summit of Benwisken, a companion peak to Benbulbin. Ley hunting is in its infancy in

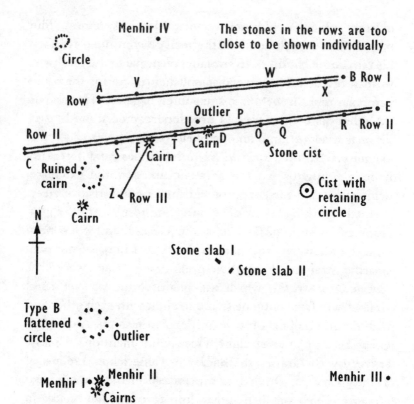

Diagram showing the stone rows at Merrivale.

Ireland and there is much to be uncovered. (See Directory: Sligo Fairy Passes.)

Prehistoric straight lines

On a smaller scale than the map ley, ancient straight alignments can be found in Britain, many of which show an intimate connection with burial places, and by inference, the spirits of the dead. Dartmoor is studded with rows of standing stones, sometimes singly and sometimes in pairs (see Plate 13). Often they pass over a burial chamber or run to or from a stone circle (see Directory: Merrivale Lines). The most famous stone rows in England can be found at Avebury in Wiltshire. The Kennet Avenue consists of a parallel pair of lines of massive sarsen stones which once ran from the Sanctuary, the site of a lost stone circle and once the site of a wooden building associated with funerary rites, to the vast henge and stone circle of Avebury itself. Only part of the Avenue can now be seen (see Plate 14). It consists of a series of straight sections and at changes of direction in the Avenue archaeologists have discovered remains of human burials (see Directory: A Solemne Walke). At Callanish, on the Isle of Lewis in the Outer Hebrides, four avenues of upright stones converge from the four quarters on a stone circle that was constructed around an earlier burial cist.

A slightly larger prehistoric linear feature is the Neolithic cursus. A fine example exists close to Stonehenge and consists of two parallel banks and ditches which run for nearly two miles and which enclose a long thin rectangular space. At the western end lies a long mound that copies the shape of a long barrow located at the eastern end of the cursus. The northern bank and ditch runs dead straight between these features. The Stonehenge cursus lies on a classic ley line (see Directory: Stonehenge Cursus). A line drawn along the northern bank and ditch passes through the nearby Cuckoo Stone, a single standing stone, and on to the centre of Woodhenge, another lost timber building like the Sanctuary, used for funerary rituals. A burial of a sacrificed girl was discovered at the centre of Woodhenge. This alignment wasn't officially recognised by archaeologists until 1947, but the publication of a book on the excavations at Woodhenge prompted Alfred Watkins to write to *The Times* on 13 August 1930.

The letter, with something of an air of resentment for the way in which his idea had, until then, been ignored by archaeologists, suggested that topographical sighting or alignment might become a useful tool in antiquarian research in identifying sites for excavation. He described his discovery on the map that the northern bank of the Stonehenge cursus aligned through the Cuckoo Stone, a prehistoric megalith. He later noticed in the excavation reports on Woodhenge that the same alignment passes straight through the centre of that newly discovered monument. The line was mentioned by the archaeologists who noted that additional postholes outside Woodhenge aligned on the Cuckoo Stone. However their line was not extended to include the Stonehenge cursus bank. The cursus clearly pointed towards an important monument and Watkins suggested that perhaps other prehistoric linear features might indicate the presence of hitherto undiscovered sites.

The Stonehenge cursus was discovered by the antiquary William Stukeley in 1723 and was so named after the Latin for racecourse. Stumped for an explanation of this strange feature, Stukeley assumed, because of its shape, that the cursus was used for horse racing. When Stukeley visited the Stonehenge cursus its banks and ditches were more prominent than they are now, but over the centuries the plough has all but obliterated them. Other cursuses have been discovered in Britain, but mostly through aerial photography where, in certain seasonal conditions, the courses of the ditches can show up as darker lines in the fields. Despite the increasing number of discoveries, no-one is any nearer to understanding what their function was. Most of them can be found near watercourses, which has prompted a connection with rituals to do with sacred rivers; they are also often found in the vicinity of other monuments, which has led some to suggest that they were part of a ritual landscape or sacred geography, the true meaning of which we can only guess at. Burials have been found by excavation at the ends of some cursuses, but often there are few artifacts found within the enclosures themselves.

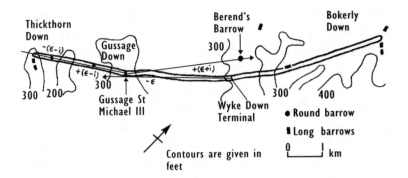

Diagram of the Dorset Cursus on Cranborne Chase, Dorset, showing the alignment of long barrows.

In *Lines on the Landscape,* Paul Devereux and Nigel Pennick examined a number of prominent British cursus monuments from the ley hunting perspective. The Dorset cursus, the largest in Britain, has several alignments to long barrows as well as a solar alignment. It is about six miles long and changes direction on its course from west to east suggesting that it may have been two cursuses joined together. The barrows, which are older than the cursuses, were probably used as sighting points to align the banks and ditches. Archaeologists accept that the link between the barrows and the cursus was deliberate, suggesting that the cursus must have been connected with practices involving ancestor worship or the veneration of the dead. More recent excavations have revealed later Bronze Age barrows linked to the cursus by straight avenues of upright timber posts showing that the sacred nature of the cursus survived several centuries and was still powerful enough to make the later inhabitants treat it with respect and reverence.

The Rudston cursus B (one of several around this Yorkshire village) is aligned on the Rudston monolith, Britain's tallest standing stone, which can be found next to the parish church. The destruction of many standing stones, the loss of many cursus monuments to the plough and development make it impossible to say whether this type of relationship between monuments was common. Other cursuses display alignments with churches. Again this may be purely fortuitous, but given that many ancient churches were built on the sites of earlier sacred places, this may indicate that a prehistoric monument once stood on the cursus alignment and that a connection between standing stones, long barrows and other monuments such as henges was common.

An incomplete picture

In each example of archaic landscape lines so far discussed it is clear that we are looking at fragments of a once complex pattern of sacred places and the pathways that link them. To further cloud the picture, successive generations, invasions and cultural changes have added to, adapted and destroyed parts of each linear system. In some places the lines survive only in the folk mind; perhaps they never were real tracks at all. Where the hard evidence does exist we are still unable to decipher the patterns we see on the ground. At best we can only project our own experiences and knowledge on to constructions made in a different time under different cultural conditions with differing expectations and beliefs. And so it was that Alfred Watkins could see no further than trade routes, the New Age believer sees only lines of energy, and flying saucer enthusiasts see the landing strips of spacecraft.

The difficulties of interpreting leys became more apparent as the Straight Track Club evolved. Opinions differed widely as to the nature of leys and Watkins was forced to comment that everyone probably had a slightly different attitude towards the question of leys. He admitted that in some cases alignments were for some purpose other than tracks.

Evidence for ley lines abounds all over the world. There is no simple explanation for any of them. From the simplicity of Watkins's idea of traders' tracks there have been subsequent discoveries of lines of kings, lines of burials, lines of religious shrines, the straight and narrow path of righteousness, lines to sources of water, lines to the rising and setting of the sun and moon, death lines and the paths of spirits and fairies. Are they all ley lines? Watkins's original definition of a ley as a sighting line of mark points set out in a dead straight line with trackways linking them together holds good for nearly all of them. But can we say with any certainty that a Neolithic Briton constructed his lines of burial mounds and stones for the same reasons that a Peruvian Indian laid out is *ceques* and *wak'as*?

Today, local authorities in Britain mark rights of way, footpaths and bridleways by a series of mark stones, finger posts and symbolic markers. Some of the old straight tracks might simply exist for the most practical reason of all – they marked the way for travellers. But we have seen that the ancient tracks that can still be traced in Britain were anything but straight. Straight tracks, where they can still be found or inferred from their mark points, seem to have had a more esoteric origin with purposes above and beyond the mundane necessity to move from A to B, and it is in this direction that modern ley hunting is now heading.

CHAPTER 6
HAUNTED HIGHWAYS:
Ghost lights and wandering spirits

Just as members of the Straight Track Club had become increasingly frustrated that a clear explanation for ley lines had not been found, so it was with the ley revivalists by the beginning of the 1980s. The notion that there might be a spirit dimension to straight landscape lines had been discussed in the Portfolios of the Straight Track Club before the War, and mention had been made of the traditional Korean belief that evil spirits could only travel in straight lines and that the native roads were deliberately engineered to twist and turn to ward off malevolent influences. The contributor noted that some ancient Korean sites had straight tracks radiating from their centres and suggested that the arrangement was intended to disperse evil spirits from the sites. The Portfolios also contain references to feng shui, the Chinese art of placement. As in Korea, the ancient Chinese held similar beliefs about the nature of spirit travel. In China, straight roads were assiduously avoided so that evil spirits or 'secret arrows' had difficulty moving around.

In *The View Over Atlantis* (1969), John Michell revived these ideas, although no great attention was paid to them at the time. Almost as an aside, one of the plates in the book shows an old footpath that runs between Bromham and Westbrook in Wiltshire. The caption refers to the many stretches of old tracks that are said to be the seasonal routes of spirits. This particular path is reputed to be haunted by a misty white figure.

Ghosts and paranormal activity are frequently associated with stretches of old (and sometimes new) roads and trackways. Perhaps an examination of some of these traditional beliefs might shed light on the nature of the old straight track.

Down to the crossroads

All roads and tracks must cross at some stage, and Alfred Watkins drew particular attention to crossroads in *The Old Straight Track*. Time and again during his map searches for leys, he encountered the 'most constant and curious experience' of finding present-day crossroads on the crossing points of his leys. Although the old straight tracks had all but disappeared, the crossing points had survived and modern roads still crossed at these points. In many cases he found that modern roads and tracks swerved more or less from his plotted straight ley, but returned to it at places which were almost always crossroads or the meeting points of other tracks. The crossing places were often still marked by ancient standing stones and mark stones or crosses. The latter, Watkins surmised, had replaced earlier unworked stones. The 'stone at the crossroads', he said, 'seems to have had a far-reaching effect on the history of religion, commerce and topography'.

No-man's land

Traditionally, the crossroads was a kind of no-man's land, neither here nor there, a place beyond the real world, a liminal space where normal physical laws did not apply. At such places it was possible to make contact with the spirit world. Wayside shrines and crosses are a common feature of crossroads in Europe, and suicides and murderers were frequently buried at such places as it was seen as unconsecrated ground, set apart from the everyday world. Such outcasts were not for heaven and were buried in a place where their spirits would be forced to wander indecisively for eternity. Burial in these places was a safeguard, but the reasons for this are unclear. Perhaps the shape of the traditional crossroads created the impression of consecrated ground, as suicides were denied normal Christian burial; perhaps it was believed that the malign spirits of the dead would disperse along the roads leading from the crossroads and not be concentrated in one spot. As a consequence, ghostly legends became attached to crossroads and they have become widely associated with magic and the appearances and activities of demons, the Devil, witches, fairies, ghosts, spirits and other paranormal phenomena.

Such folk beliefs have survived into the 20th century and travelled to the New World. A famous tale concerns the legendary blues guitarist Robert Johnson, who 'went down to the crossroads', as the song goes, and traded his soul to the Devil in exchange for his renowned guitar skills. The price was high and Johnson was to die young and penniless.

The crossings of paths is a specific area of interest for those who collect stories of paranormal activity, especially sightings of ghosts or spirits. Such sightings and other paranormal events often take place along ancient highways and especially at the crossings of such highways. If it can be accepted that ghosts move along the paths, then it stands to reason that they must meet – perhaps even correspond in some way – at crossroads. Whether these tales tell of real events or whether they are colourful evidence of a perceived belief in both the existence of ghosts and spirits and their behaviour, does not directly concern us here. The importance for ley hunters is that the stories exist at all and what they say about the landscape and our relationship to it. The traditional associations

of the crossroads with spirits and ghosts can be found all over
Europe and the British Isles, as well as in Greece, India,
Japan, and amongst Native Americans and Mongols, which
suggests that the origins of these beliefs must have had some
basis in real human experience.

Crossroads were believed to be haunted by various entities
that took delight in leading travellers astray. Stories abound
from Europe of the many encounters between ordinary folk
and spirits at crossroads and the highways leading to and
from them. German lore tells of a ghostly rider who haunts
a crossroads in Schleswig and prevents people from passing
by sticking his horse's neck out into the road. A legend from
Pomerania tells of the encounter between a traveller and a
shadowy figure at a crossroads. The apparition follows the
poor fellow home and begins to haunt his house. Eventually
the man speaks to the ghost who asks him to accompany him
to a churchyard and pray for his release from his purgatory.
(See also Plate 11.)

All Hallows Eve is a favourite time for spirits to gather
at crossroads, a time where the boundaries between this
world and the Otherworld are most likely to be breached.
Welsh lore attests to this annual gathering at every crossroads. In European lore the gathering Hallowe'en spirits
walk in procession to visit the homes of their relatives. These
ghostly processions can be seen if you stand at a crossroads
and rest your chin on a forked stick. Other stories tell of how
to gain access to spirits, ghosts and witches at crossroads by
performing elaborate rituals. Danish lore instructs those who
wish to contact the Otherworld to stand at a crossroads
within a rectangle formed by cart tracks and call out the name
of the ghost you wish to speak with. These encounters were
usually for some specific purpose and often to find out who
was going to die. Various legends tell of hearing the names
of those about to die and the wind blowing over the feet of
the corpses on its way to the houses of the doomed.

In Britain, folk memory still records the belief in spirits and methods of protection against them. Spirit 'sweeping' was practised in the Isle of Man; Bernadette Thomas records in *The Ley Hunter* that as a child she was told that evil spirits could be dispersed if she went to a crossroads at midnight and swept the intersection clear with a broom.

Supernatural highways

In order to gather at crossroads, spirits must travel there by some route or other. Tales of haunted highways abound in folklore, as do tales of ghostly funeral processions, phantom coaches and strange lights. Many of these stories of hauntings along old roads and tracks feature movement in straight lines, which may provide significant clues to unravelling the mystery of leys and lines on the landscape.

Hauntings and paranormal activity are not confined to old roads and tracks, and modern folk tales bear a remarkable similarity to traditional legends. This suggests that the source of many of these stories, where they cannot be shown to be fabrications, may well be based on real, unexplained events. Here follows a selection of tales of ghostly goings on in roads around my home county of Gloucestershire.

The Reverend Harry Cheales, former vicar of Wyck Rissington and noted student of the supernatural, drew attention to the large number of accidents, some fatal, that have taken place on the junction between the old A436 road between Andoversford and Stow-on-the-Wold and the modern A40 bypass between Cheltenham and Oxford. He suggested that supernatural influences might be the cause of the trouble. Six bodies from the late Roman period were found close to a spot where the road crosses the River Coln – an odd 'blind spot' – at which approaching vehicles seem to disappear and then re-emerge when almost on top of the crossroads. This was not a usual Roman burial ground and the skeletal abnormality of the remains and the shallowness with which they were buried suggests great haste in internment. The added belief that a gallows once stood on the spot suggests that this 'black spot' might have been one of those liminal spaces where paranormal activity is more likely to happen.

Further west along the same road, the stretch from the Salperton-Compton Abdale crossroads is also accident-prone. It was part of the main salt-way from Droitwich (Worcestershire) to Lechlade (Wiltshire) and beyond and was probably in use from Iron Age times or before. Many of the accidents have involved single vehicles that left the road and overturned on verges or plunged into adjacent fields. A ghostly horse and trap is well known in the area. It has been seen on the main road and it has been speculated that the accidents were due to drivers swerving to avoid the apparition.

Close to the Pusedown Inn on the A40 a track leaves the road eastwards, keeping to the north of Hampnett village and crossing the Fosse Way to Farmington before rejoining the main road. The track was once an alternative to the main coaching road and two sightings have been reported of a coach and four emerging from this track at the Pusedown end, crossing the A40 and continuing into the belt of wood-land opposite. The apparition was lifelike and it was even possible to discern the colour of the horses. The sighting of stagecoaches is an extremely common tradition.

In 1972 a driver was travelling in his delivery van along the A417 Ermine Street at early dusk. He had passed the Highwayman pub and had reached the approach to the turning to Syde village when a coach drawn by four white horses crossed the road obliquely some 15 yards ahead of him. Ermine Street is a Roman road, with possibly prehistoric origins, which links Gloucester and Cirencester. This road, like many Roman constructions, is a series of straight sections linked together by bends and curves necessitated by changes of contour. This particular incident occurred on a dead straight stretch.

Such phantom encounters on modern roads are common and bear uncanny similarities to more traditional stories in their locations. Along with crossroads, fords and bridges are other favourite haunts of apparitions. In their survey of modern mysteries, Janet and Colin Bord report the case of school headmaster Bill Hopkins who was driving home one night in May 1973. As he approached the Red Bridge, an old railway bridge, on the road between Llanidloes and Newtown in Powys, a girl stepped out of the hedge into his path. Thinking he was about to hit the girl he braked and was amazed and shaken to find that there was no impact as he seemingly passed through the apparition; she was quite visible afterwards in his rear view mirror. The publicity surrounding the report of this case revealed that a number of other people had had similar experiences when driving across Red Bridge. Other such incidents have been reported on the A12 near Hopton in Essex, where a late night driver braked and swerved to avoid hitting a spectral figure in the middle of the road, only to pass straight through it.

Spirit paths, secret tunnels and black dogs

These few examples are relatively modern, but there are hundreds of older tales that tell of the linear movement of ghosts, phantom coaches, headless horses, black dogs and so on. While some may have only a spurious connection with an old road or track, others provide tantalising clues to link ghost sightings and paranormal phenomena with leys. It is evidence such as this that has led to a fresh interpretation of Watkins's original discovery. Even when the idea that leys were some form of 'Earth energy' zapping between standing stones was popular the notion of spirit lines surfaced briefly before being subsumed in the 'Earth energy' ideas of post-war ley hunters.

In the mid-1970s the pioneer Earth Mysteries writer John Michell wrote of the legend that attributed to the feet of angels the old tracks that lead from one stone cross to another across the wastes of Dartmoor. In historical times the tracks were retrodden by saints, pilgrims and pedlars and in this way were transformed from spirit paths into footpaths. Networks of these routes can, he said, be discovered in all countries where they are used at festivals in connection with ceremonies, for ritual journeys and pilgrimages, and for funeral routes or corpse paths. Many are now lost, but the memory of them remains in the legends of underground tunnels linking ancient sites and burial places.

In the past, ley hunters have often come across legends of underground tunnels and passages which have been looked upon as possible folk memories of old buried trackways and paths linking places with churches and ancient sites. Watkins excavated several of these 'lost' tracks during his investigations. The link between legendary long distance tunnels and spirit paths seems to be a universal theme in folklore; an underground passage often indicates a real secret route above ground.

One such legend is that of the Black Abbot of Prestbury, Gloucestershire, reputedly England's most haunted village. The Black Abbot may be seen at Easter, Christmas and on All Saint's Day. His walk starts in the church at Prestbury, continues through the churchyard and ends at Reform Cottage (a weatherboarded house dating from the 16th century). Paranormal activity is supposed to occur in the cottage when the old monk is about. The cottage garden is said to lie over the burial ground of the monks who came to Prestbury from Llanthony Abbey in Gloucester, and a secret passageway is supposed to link the cottage with the church.

Another legend is that of the Langston Arms hotel in Kingham in Oxfordshire, which has a reputation for hauntings. A number of occurrences took place in 1964 where a ghost appeared to the landlord or the customers every ten days or so in the form of a white shape that resembled the figure of a nun in a head-dress. Shuffling footsteps and strange sounds like someone coughing often preceded the appearance. The building is only 200 years old, but the foundations are earlier and there is a story of a bricked up secret passageway that led to Bruern Abbey. Another tunnel is supposed to link Tangley Hall with the Abbey, four miles away.

Other examples include legends of underground passages in Moreton-in-Marsh, Gloucestershire (Manor Holme Hotel to the church), Northleach, Gloucestershire (Gaggle Cottage to the church), and Great Wolford, Warwickshire, where a secret passage leads from the Fox and Hounds pub to the nearby church, along which the deceased were supposedly carried. Many years ago it was said that the bodies waiting for burial would be laid in what is now the dining room of the inn. Subsequent hauntings have been reported from the pub. Even after their everyday uses had been abandoned, the reputation of these old pathways survived in their legends as spirit paths and the haunts of fairies and ghosts. There is a notorious place close to Ilmington in Warwickshire on the Stratford Road at the crossroads by Bruton Barn where farmers returning from Stratford market late at night would be held up. Their horses would refuse to budge and they would sit for an hour or more. This was supposed to have been the burial place of a highwayman who was laid to rest with a stake driven through his heart.

A spectral funeral procession is apparently to be seen speeding through hedges and ditches from Weston-sub-Edge on the edge of the Cotswolds to Bretforton churchyard, a route that follows an old burial path; a phantom white calf has been seen on the road to Ettington in Warwickshire,

Plate 8: A classic Watkinsian ley. Castle mound, tree-lined avenue and Old Radnor Church, Herefordshire, in alignment.

Plate 9: (left) A straight track almost 20 miles long crosses the hilly landscape of the Bolivian Andes at a height of over 13,000 feet.

Plate 10: (below) Two dead straight paths run up a hill-side to hilltop shrines in a remote Andean village.

Plate 11: (above) The snow-covered death road leading to a cemetery near Gtodowo in Pomerania, Poland. To the left is a large wooden cross, to the right a standing stone. The bush behind the stone is traditionally decorated with strips of red and white cloth, left to please the nature spirits.

Plate 12: (right) One of the three *Doodwegen* or death roads crossing the Westerheide heath between Hilversum and Laren in the Netherlands.

Plate 13: (left) One of the stone rows at Merrivale on Dartmoor, Devon. The triangular stone in the foreground is the 'blocking stone' set across the path between the stones.

Plate 14: (below) The Kennet Avenue, Avebury, Wiltshire. Concrete bollards mark the locations of missing megaliths.

which is also haunted by an old woman wearing a sun-bonnet and carrying a basket. A Roman burial place was discovered close to this road.

A manuscript dating from the 1850s mentions a pool at Hoarwithy in Herefordshire, said to be haunted. The pool was close to where 'the Bierless Road falls into the Hereford Road'. Local historian Heather Hurley says that Bierless Road (which no longer exists, but whose line can still be traced) was a corpse way leading to a burial ground where the corpses of suicides, paupers and vagrants were laid to rest.

At Barton-on-the-Heath in Warwickshire there is a bend in the road to Kitebrook where a willow tree is supposed to mark the spot where a highwayman was hanged. His ghost haunts the road. A 'grey lady' haunts another spot further along the road. At Lyme Park Hall, between Whaley Bridge and Stockport in Cheshire, a ghostly funeral procession haunts the one and a quarter mile drive between the park gates and the house. The cortège bears the body of Sir Piers Leigh, a knight who served Henry V in his campaign in France. Another north country road ghost can be found near Raby Castle, south-west of Bishop Auckland. A phantom horseman roams the lanes near West Auckland, riding a white horse towards Hamsterley Forest, where he gradually disappears as if the horse was galloping into the ground. Finally, 12 miles from the Canterbury end of the Pilgrim's Way, an ancient trackway with a grand tradition of haunt-ings, near the crossroads of the A253 Ramsgate to Canterbury road and the A266 going south from Margate, there used to be a burial ground and a gibbet. At night a glowing light moves along the road, flickers across the junction and momentarily takes on the shape of a robed figure.

In their study of English leys in the late 1970s Paul Devereux and Ian Thompson recorded ghost sighting legends on 17 of their 41 surveyed examples and suggested that the link was probably between ghosts and the sites on the leys rather than with the leys themselves. But until we can say with any surety what a ley is this will have to remain an open question.

Despite the randomness of many of these sightings, attempts have been made in the past to find some kind of order to paranormal sightings within a localised area. A type of ghostly line, which has been recorded in folklore, is that of the phantom black dog. In Portfolio 11 of the Straight Track Club archive Barbara Carbonnel writes:

'For some time I have had in my mind that some of the traditional "walks" or "haunts" of ghosts and spectres might be connected with the straight track alignments. And I think I have found at least one instance of one, of which I give the particulars. There is in this neighbourhood – mid-Devon – a tradition of a black dog – a spectre – which is seen at night on certain roads, and the apparition is spoken of locally as 'The Black Dog of Torrington'. Torrington is about 12 miles distant from the point where the spectre is said to come from, and on first hearing this tale, I tried to see if any line could be found which would go from Copleston Cross – the starting point – to Torrington and yet pass through the several points at which the spectre is said to have been seen. I do not pretend to have searched the full extent of the line exhaustively but I have done a considerable part of it and I think the result may prove very interesting and the details I propose to give will show that the line does lie right through the points where the dog is said to have been known to pass.'

Theo Brown was able to add further such Black Dog lines to the area. He mentioned a Cornish Black Dog line running from Liskeard to Launceston and another, curving, line running from Liskeard to Tavistock.

In 1977 the Earth Mysteries writer, John Michell, recounted an old tale of a Black Dog seen in 1907 by a Somerset man, near Budleigh Hill. This fiery-eyed apparition was seen to run along the road until it came to a spot where a stream passed under it. When it reached that spot the dog shot up into the air in a flash of fire. A common belief was that such phantoms could not abide running water. A similar tale from Dartmoor tells of a farmer who chased a phantom Black Dog to a crossroads where it seemed to explode in a blinding flash. Away from the connection with water and the crossroads, another account of a Black Dog sighting concerns that of a phantom creature that rushes at midnight through a Devonshire village along a road from the church, demolishing a corner of a schoolhouse, or seeming to demolish it because although falling masonry can be heard, no actual damage is done. In Lyme Regis in Dorset, however, the corner of an inn known as The Black Dog was reputedly knocked down by a phantom Black Dog. Black Dog sightings are also traditionally associated with churchyards and stretches of old roads. In Scotland the Black Dog is known as *cu sith* and is believed to travel in straight lines along certain roads, its sighting being a warning of impending ill luck and even death. A straight track on the north Somerset coast is referred to as Death Mile because locals believed it to be haunted by a Black Dog that brings death to whoever sees it.

More recently researchers have been looking out for folklore evidence that points directly to a straight line connection between sightings of paranormal events. Hidden passageways, which ley hunters often took as indicators of old alignments, can be found in the suburbs of Bristol. Local researcher Phil Quinn, writing in *The Ley Hunter*, mentions a tower on the highest point in the Old Forest of Kingswood, all that survives of the now destroyed King John's Hunting Lodge. It was said that a secret tunnel ran for 2.5km northeast to Staple Hill House. Another, unrelated, folk tale tells of a warrior on a white horse who would charge through the gates of the Lodge and gallop across country to the Forest Pool where it promptly disappeared. When plotted on the map, Forest Pool sits in direct alignment between the Lodge and Staple Hill House following the line of the secret passage.

Quinn also discovered another example at Hinton Charterhouse, North Somerset, where a secret tunnel is believed to run from the ruined Carthusian Priory, under the parish church and on to the medieval George Inn, built by the monks and one of England's most ancient hostelries. As the passage runs through the grounds of Hinton House it crosses an area haunted by the ghost of a young girl and a footpath that mirrors the route of the tunnel is paved with large stones and has been called the Monk's Way. Quinn asks whether this might once have been a sacred route used by seen and unseen souls.

Taking our lead from the examples of spirit travel quoted in the early days of the ley hunting revival of the 1960s, we can surmise that an explanation for some leys might be the spirit path. These often invisible paths have survived in British folklore via the phantom funeral procession, the wandering ghostly monk, the spectral horseman and ghostly lights, their courses frequently recorded as routes to and from churches, crossroads and burial places. Sometimes these spirit ways have a physical counterpart, by way of an old paved track, or can be successfully plotted on the map to show their straightness. Many of Watkins's leys incorporated old trackways leading to ancient churches and crosses. He records two specific cases where he found straight trackways sighted directly on churchyard crosses – Monk's Walk, an ancient avenue at Much Marcle, Herefordshire, and at

Kingstone where a straight piece of ancient lane paved with cobbles aligns with the cross in the churchyard. Indeed, many of his leys were almost exclusively lines of churches, giving the lie to the idea that leys were prehistoric in origin and much ammunition to his detractors. Classic examples of church leys can be found at Bristol, Oxford and York (see Directory: York Minster Ley and Oxford City Leys).

Ghost paths

The rekindling of interest in the folklore aspects of ley hunting and the revival of the spirit line idea has encouraged researchers from Britain and mainland Europe to re-examine their local folklore and legends to see if any further clues to the straight spirit line might be found. The German Fortean researcher Ulrich Magin has been a regular contributor to *The Ley Hunter* for many years, and his discovery of the German *Geisterwege*, or ghost paths, has given a boost to the spirit line theory of leys. Magin found a reference to *Geisterwege* in the *Handwörterbuch des Deutschen Aberglaubens* (*The Handbook of German Folklore*):

> GHOST PATH. Ghost paths are always in the same place, on them one meets with ghosts quite often. The paths, with no exception, always run in a straight line over mountains and valleys and through marshes. In the towns they pass the houses closely or go right through them. The paths end or originate at a cemetery. This idea may stem from the ancient custom of driving a corpse along a special dead man's road, therefore the way or road was believed to have the same characteristics as a cemetery, it is a place where spirits of the deceased thrive.' (Trans. Ulrich Magin)

The German *Geisterwege* shares several characteristics with the Irish fairy pass and suggests a common origin of ideas. Both are invisible and both are permanent routes for the passage of ghosts or spirits. In both cases, too, it is believed to be extremely unlucky, even dangerous, to block the spirit path. Magin, writing in *The Ley Hunter*, recounts the tale of the '*Leichenflugbahn*' or 'Flightpath of the corpses' in the town of Ragnit (or Nemen, as it is now known), situated on the Memel river in Russia. *Leichen* is German for corpses and *Flugbahn* is a flight path, a word that modern Germany reserves for aircraft. The folk story is retold in Christa Hinze's and Ulf Diederich's book *Ostpreußische Sagen* (*Folktales of East Prussia*).

Ragnit has two cemeteries, one for the German population and one for the Lithuanian. Traditionally, no shrub or tree, house or wall is allowed on a line drawn between the two cemeteries, because it was believed that such obstructions would hinder the movement of the dead. Friends who had since died would visit each other on stormy nights, flying through the air from one cemetery to the other. The souls of the dead fly close to the ground and will not tolerate any obstructions that stand higher than an ell (this is a traditional unit of measure derived from the distance between the elbow and fingertips). A legend tells of a foreigner who, ignoring the warnings of local people, built a house on the south side of the town on the invisible line between the cemeteries. Before the completion of the roof a storm in the night brought down the walls of the house. However, makeshift huts on either side remained standing despite the storm. The builder, embarrassed that he had ignored the warnings of the locals, decided to defy the flying spirits and he rebuilt the house. Again, before the roof could be finished there was another stormy night. Once again the house was destroyed. This time the builder relented and built his house a short distance away. There it remained unscathed and is still standing today.

The flightpath is very precisely defined. Another Ragnit man with second sight wanted to erect a shed south of the town. He could see the flying spirits and marked their route with a stick so that he might build away from the line. In the event he must have misjudged the true line for after another stormy night he found the corner of the gable had been torn down. He set about re-erecting the shed a few feet away and suffered no further damage. However, it is said that a small roof pin still projects into the flightpath and the owner has to replace it about a hundred times a year.

While the word used for the flightpath of the corpses, *Strich* (strip), can mean 'land' as well as 'line', there is little doubt that the path must have been straight. It was precisely defined and narrow, and the Ragnit man who could see the spirits needed only one marker to define its course.

Magin notes that all the references he has so far unearthed on the subject of non-physical straight lines such as the *Leichenflugbahn* all predate Watkins as well as Watkins's German contemporaries, and therefore indicate that the tales cannot be based on the modern concept of ley lines but must relate to some older tradition. John Michell, writing in *Phenomena*, mentions a similar traditional path. The Wild Troop of Rodenstein in Germany is a disagreeable force that steers a straight course between the two lofty castles of Rodenstein and Schnellert, blasting all in its path.

The spectral, nocturnal procession of huntsmen, ghosts of the dead and their horses and hounds is known throughout Europe. The Wild Hunt, as it is called, has its origins in Norse and Teutonic mythologies where, on stormy nights, Odin, in the guise of a mounted huntsman, was said to take to the skies with a pack of spectral dogs and lay the countryside to waste. Any poor soul unfortunate enough to encounter the Wild Hunt during one of its jaunts would be transported to a foreign land. The Wild Hunt takes to the air on specific dates and in Germany, at least, Ulrich Magin has recorded the routes of some of the Wild Hunts. In any particular area the Hunt often follows the same route, sometimes causing damage to buildings, and in one incident in Baden-Württemburg, it left a visible track, but it is not recorded whether or not the path of the Wild Hunt is straight.

To 'ley' a ghost?

Here lies the difficulty faced by today's ley hunters. Many old stories may give locations, times and details of events, but they frequently fail to describe accurately the nature of the ghostly route. This may be because the routes always varied, or perhaps because it was common knowledge that spirits flew in straight lines so it wasn't necessary to state the obvious. Nevertheless, in some cases the straight aspect of spirit movement is quite categorical and further investigation can provide clues as to the route of a particular ghost on its nocturnal travels.

It would be easy to jump to the conclusion that the existence of a ley in a particular location was a good enough reason to believe that ghosts and spirits are likely to be encountered on or near them. There is no real evidence for this idea, though the modern belief that leys are some form of energy line has led to all manner of speculation regarding the power of certain points on a ley and the interaction of energies at these special locations being responsible for paranormal activity and the appearance of ghosts. Without any real evidence this has to remain speculative.

Many ghostly tales were probably contrived in relatively recent times for all manner of purposes and do not relate to real events at all. But the idea of ghosts and spirits is so widespread and enduring that it suggests a real physical reason for the development of the idea in the first place. Certainly, paranormal events have occurred and been witnessed that are place-related; people have seen apparitions or ghosts, others have had very real experiences that lead them to believe that the spirit world is not fantasy but an aspect of reality that is denied to all but a favoured few. The durability of traditional beliefs in fairies and Otherworld beings and the continuance of practices related to those beliefs testifies to some genuine truth.

Given that a proportion of ghost stories and legends have a basis in real events, how does that relate to the straight landscape line, if at all? A spirit could take any route on its way from A to B. People will take the straightest path between two points, but are constrained by hills and rivers, valleys and vegetation, and naturally their paths are forced to take a winding course. Spirits, on the other hand, have no such constraints and flight between two points is perceived to be straight. Random courses should be the norm. Straight paths are unusual, so where straightness is specified in these tales then it must be significant. This straightness must come from real human experience, possibly from witnessing the passage of spirits, either in waking reality, in dreams, or in the subconscious experience of the Otherworld. There is no other rational explanation for the worldwide belief in straight spirit flight.

The ley, then, is not responsible for paranormal events. On the contrary, the occurrence of moving spirits and ghosts is *what defines the line*. In most cases these lines are invisible and recoverable only through the points at which the events occur or by fragments of the ghostly linear journey between them – not a dissimilar database to that which presented itself to Alfred Watkins when he first discovered the old straight track. The spirit line is but one aspect of landscape linearity and a specific one in that *it is invisible*. In some cultures these invisible Otherworld roads have been paralleled in the physical world by the making of real tracks and roads for ceremonial and ritual purposes that follow or

mark them and which relate to the worship of spirits and the
fear of the dead. These real tracks can be identified in the
phenomena of the death road and the funeral path and these
and other ceremonial straight pathways will be examined in
chapter 7.

CHAPTER 7
SPIRIT WAYS AND DEATH ROADS

It seems that Watkins stumbled upon something of far greater significance than a decayed system of straight track-ways, a fact that became obvious to members of the Straight Track Club when a simple explanation of ley lines failed to appear. Some insightful and innovative suggestions were made by different members, but were forgotten following the demise of the club. Some of these ideas, particularly the connection between leys and the movement of evil spirits along straight roads survived into the post-war ley hunting revival and have sustained up to the present day. It is a short step from phantom funeral parties to death and burial, and this chapter examines the evidence for a connection between death rituals, traditional funeral routes and ley lines.

If ancient straight tracks and roads are to be associated with the movement of spirits and ghosts, then it is a logical step to associate the same routes with the movement of the dead. Already we have seen instances of phantom funeral processions on ancient tracks or travelling between churches and churchyards. Death, burial and the spirit world are inter-twined in folklore and common factors are the road, the track and the crossroads. Not surprisingly, many superstitions, customs and ceremonies have evolved that surround the apparently simple act of carrying a corpse to burial.

Curious funeral customs

Crossroads played an important part in the rituals surrounding funerals and burials. Watkins remarked, in passing, on the curious tradition of laying down the coffin on route to the churchyard at a crossroads and saying a prayer. This custom was still practised in his day. He mentioned the 'Funeral Stone' at Brilley in Herefordshire, which stood outside the churchyard gate; traditionally the coffin was carried around the stone three times before being taken into the church. This was believed to prevent the Devil from getting the dead man's soul. Although he didn't pursue this line of enquiry any further, it will become apparent that the connection between death, burial and the straight route goes a long way to explaining some of Watkins' own leys.

Other folklore references talk about the remarkable practice of 'bumping' the coffin. In some places the coffin was bumped against the pedestal of every wayside cross passed on the journey and also on the walls of the church when the corpse was removed after the funeral service. In Ireland it was thought necessary for the funeral party to proceed three times around *any* church that was passed on the way to the graveyard.

By way of coincidence, another tradition is linked to the passing of a funeral party over a bridge. Previously we have noted the connection between bridges and ghostly phenomena. Custom forbade singing or the playing of musical instruments while a funeral party was crossing a bridge. Such places, like crossroads, were considered, at certain specific times, to be liminal places where the veil between this world and the next was the thinnest. Perhaps here, the silence gave some form of protection to either the mourners or the deceased on the final journey. In some areas it was considered extremely dangerous to take a corpse twice across a bridge from the house where the death had taken place – to the church and back again to the burial place, for instance. If this rule was broken it was thought that the bridge would break. In order to avoid this, chapels were frequently built on the bridge itself, although the origin of this custom is not very clear. Perhaps this is an attempt to explain away a forgotten earlier tradition that crossing a bridge, or water, was a method of ensuring that the soul of the deceased would not be able to return to haunt his house. However, crossing the same bridge twice might have lessened the effect or even brought the spirit back with the mourners.

Another traditional belief concerns the corpse candle or corpse light. These are mysterious lights which bob along above the ground or float in the air at night. Beliefs about them vary from one place to another. Invariably they were thought to warn of the imminent death of someone in the locality; it might be the observer or someone they know. Sometimes corpse lights stop at the house of someone who is about to die. In Hampshire the lights are said to accompany the souls of the departed and are extinguished when the souls leave the earth. Ghostly funerals are said to accompany some of the lights. Writing in *The History of Kington*, at the end of the 19th century, Richard Parry noted that country folk believed that a corpse candle preceded the death of a person in the neighbourhood. They also believed that it marked the route of the funeral from the house of the deceased to the churchyard and, indeed, to the very spot where the body was to be laid in the grave. The corpse candle is closely related to another class of ghostly light, *'ignis fatuus'*, also known as the 'will o' the wisp', 'jack o'lantern' or 'fetch light'. Perhaps they are all examples of the same natural phenomenon. Their frequent appearance in churchyards and marshy ground led to the belief that they were a device of evil spirits designed to draw human beings from the road into danger and even death.

In other cultures worldwide, mysterious lights such as

these are regarded as the disembodied spirits of ancestors. It has been suggested by Paul Devereux that these lights are related to a largely unrecognised natural phenomenon, which he has termed 'Earth lights'. These lights are intimately connected with the local topography, are related to seismic activity and cluster around areas of local geological faulting. There is evidence to suggest that Earth lights have an electromagnetic dimension which can have an effect on the state of consciousness of anyone unfortunate enough to come into close contact with them, causing hallucinations, time slips and unconsciousness. This would explain the traditional belief in their intimate relationship with the spirit world, premonition and paranormal phenomena. Their appearance in remote areas alongside a lonely trackway or isolated churchyard would also suggest a connection with the dead.

Parry also mentions the practice of putting down the corpse for a few moments at a crossroads and for the mourners all to stand still. He attempts an explanation for this custom in the words of the Dean of Hereford, who remarked that 'Diana, who was so-called upon Earth, and Luna in heaven, was styled Hecate in hell – and that her statues were always placed where three ways met. The dread which the ancients felt of her in those places, may not unreasonably be supposed to have been handed down to succeeding generations – and the custom to have survived the motive for the practice.'

In *The Folklore of the Welsh Border*, Jacqueline Simpson makes note of the custom of setting down the coffin at certain spots on its way to burial, or the need to carry it around some particular tree or stone, or to turn it around before entering the churchyard. As late as 1930, in Trelleck, Monmouthshire, the coffin bearers would pause to set down the coffin as soon as they came in sight of the church. In earlier times, funeral parties coming from Park House to Trelleck church used to carry the coffin around the stump of an old wayside cross, while others crossing Penault Common used to stop and sing a psalm while the coffin was rested on a stone bench under a certain oak tree. At Pembridge in Herefordshire, coffins were always brought to the church by a roundabout route, halting for a few moments at each crossroads and then carried sunwise around the church before entering. This protective measure may have had the similar effect of ensuring the Devil could not take the soul of the deceased.

Another custom related to previous suggestions that Watkins' sighting mounds were the result of successive travellers laying down a stone on route along an ancient trackway, is that recorded at Rhayader and a few other places in Radnorshire. The mourners in a funeral procession would each carry a small pebble and as they passed a certain spot they would throw their pebbles on to a pile of stones left from previous funerals. These cairns were still being added to at funerals as late as 1910.

Hay strewing, straw lore and sweeping

Amongst the traditional customs connected to movement in straight lines are those to do with hay strewing and the use of straw to ward off evil spirits. Two examples of hay strewing were unearthed by Paul Devereux and Andrew York in 1974, though their relevance to ley hunting then was only hinted at. Last performed in the 19th century, this custom involved the collection of hay on a particular day from a special part of a meadow. From there it was carried by hand in a straight line to the now demolished Enderby church in Leicestershire, where it was scattered along the nave. Devereux and York located the site of the meadow and discovered four unrecorded standing stones and a half-mile section of straight unsurfaced road aligned on the meadow.

They found a similar tradition at Braunstone, also in Leicestershire, where hay had to be gathered from a meadow in nearby Aylestone and taken 'as the crow flies' to Braunstone church.

Similar traditions were unearthed by the artist and Earth Mysteries researcher John Palmer. In France, as late as the 13th century, straw rather than hay was spread on the floor of buildings where it was believed to ward off sorcery. In Flanders and Holland crosses made of straw bushels, tied together with three bands, used to be deposited to identify the route to be taken by a funeral party: at the door of the deceased's house, at a crossroads on route and inside the church. The custom of laying straw in church was known at Gent in Flanders, and in the city of Antwerp the laying of straw was required by a law decreed in 1472.

In West Flanders the ancient custom of laying a cross made of straw in front of the house of a deceased person was thought to prevent the spirit from re-entering. At the town of Staden, Germany, four bushels were used, each laid flat on the ground, and a brick was placed on the crossroads. Before 1870, small crosses made of straw were hung at the door and windows of the house if the deceased was a child. Bushels of straw were also put on both sides of the coffin upon the bier or burial cart. Upon the return of the funeral party the corpse straw or *lijkstro* was placed on the four corners of a nearby crossroads; it was believed that the straw provided protection from malignant influences and sorcery. The custom of laying the dead on straw existed in Friesland, Limburg, North Brabant, the Velhuwe region, and at Staphorst and Giethoorn, all in the Netherlands. Small straw crosses were laid at crossroads in Damme, in Flanders, and in Eegem and Gits. In northern France, crosses of straw and wood were hung at wayside crosses or chapels.

At the death of a landowner in eastern Zeeuws in Flanders, the road from his house to the church was laid with straw. In the region of Dion-le-Val this custom was only carried out for important people and was used in 1913 at the burial of Baron Craninckx, and in 1930 for the burial of Lord de Villiers, owner of Beausart Castle. In the Land van Waas in Flanders, the street was strewn with the 'last' straw, and straw from funerals in Germany used to be dropped at the crossroads.

Another custom, often related to the laying of straw, was sweeping. A north European folk tradition held that disused paths could be swept free of haunting spirits with a special flail. There was also a connection with death as it was traditional to sweep the room after the coffin had been taken out. In Thüringen in Germany, salt was sprinkled in the room after sweeping and the broom was disposed of in a field or in the churchyard. Similarly, the old Prussians held a death meal for the family after a burial to which the soul of the deceased and those of their ancestors were invited, and after the meal the priest would sweep the room with a broom. Similar customs can be found in other parts of the world, which suggest a conceptual link with those of northern Europe. In Borneo, for instance, the spirit of the deceased is feasted for four days on rice, after which brushing takes place and the food plates are broken. In the Andean villages of South America, strips of village plazas are swept to create 'sacred space' before the parading of a saint's statue. Archaeologists and anthropologists also believe that archaic landscape lines in South America, such as the lines on the pampa at Nazca in Peru, were similarly swept. In Columbia, the Kogi Indians ritually sweep the ancient stone-paved spirit roads built by their ancestors.

Dead straight

What of the funeral routes themselves? The old funeral path may hold the key to the explanation of some of Watkins's alignments, particularly those of ancient churches. The trigger to this intriguing line of enquiry for ley hunters was the unlikely discovery of dead straight roads in Holland, which were used for the carrying of corpses to burial during the Middle Ages.

During his research into the blue stones and circular mosaics that mark the geomantic centres of old Dutch towns, John Palmer noticed the common occurrence of roads that had been laid out by medieval surveyors. These old roads had a prescribed width, according to the uses to which they were put, and surveyors and travelling magistrates regularly inspected them. Among these roads were common public footpaths, mill roads, bride ways or marriage roads, church roads, cart tracks, field roads and roads for agricultural use, general purpose highways and main roads, and death roads.

Palmer found stretches of old minor roads still in existence in some places and notable examples of *Doodwegen* or death roads. These roads were specifically used to transport the deceased to burial. On Westerheide, a heath between Laren and Hilversum in north Holland, he discovered three absolutely straight roads converging on the chapel at the isolated St Janskershof (St John's cemetery) (see Plate 12). The Westerheide is peppered with Neolithic and Bronze Age barrows and is crossed by the Old Postroad and three *Doodwegen*. The death roads are thought to date from medieval times. One of them, the road from 's-Graveland, is believed to have been laid out in 1643. The other two are believed to be older, but their exact age is unknown. In addition, a stretch of the old *Varkensdrift* still exists along which pigs were driven to market; an equivalent of the old English drove road. The cemetery of St John is still in use although the present chapel is only a hundred years old. It replaced an earlier chapel dating from the 1600s (See Directory: Three Dutch Death Roads).

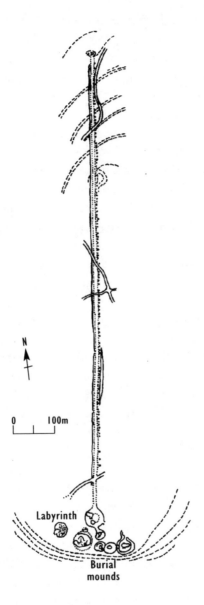

The death road at Rösaring, Lassa, southern
Sweden, running dead straight for over 540
metres to a group of Bronze, Iron and Viking
Age burial mounds.

Further research led Palmer to a law introduced in AD 784 where the council of Paderborn could serve the death penalty for the cremation of the deceased and for the burial of the ashes within pagan barrows. It was decreed that bodies had to be buried in church cemeteries. In addition, certain routes had to be followed to get them there. The Oath Formula demanded that the mourners carrying a coffin to burial had to swear that their corpse roads were in good order and that they had adhered to the straight road when carrying the coffin to burial. In Twente, Holland, these roads were maintained in good order until about 1800. The locals called this road variously *Doodenweg* (death road), *Lykweg* (corpse road) and *Spokenweg* (ghost road). Palmer notes that at the village of Neede it was, until recently, still considered improper if the burial procession took a short cut or a minor road to get to the cemetery.

Following these discoveries ley hunters in Britain started to search out examples of possible 'spirit paths' and 'death roads'. Traditions of special roads or paths dedicated to the transport of corpses for burial are numerous in the British Isles. They are called variously funeral paths, corpse ways, burial roads and coffin lines. The pages of obscure folklore books were scoured for references to these medieval death roads with surprising results.

Funeral paths and corpse ways

A notable belief was that if a corpse was carried over private land on its way to burial, it automatically established a right of way, but this has no foundation in English law. Ancient Roman law, however, prevented landowners from excluding access to traditional burial places. In the Hebrides the peasants used force to prevent any attempts to close the short cuts from the burial grounds to the sea, which the dead were supposed to use when they went to bathe.

When corpses were brought from outlying hamlets and farms for burial in the nearest parish church, the customary road or path taken by funerals was the Church Road, or sometimes the Corpse Way or Corpse Gate. Other names included Burial Lane and, in the case of an old corpse way on the outskirts of Stratford-upon-Avon in Warwickshire, 'Berrin Road', a dialect corruption of Burying Road. In the villages these roads may well have been proper paved roads, but further afield the paths crossed over the fields and were never ploughed over (see Plate 7). It was considered unlucky to use any other route for funerals, as it was believed that to do so would prevent the deceased from resting in the grave. Despite the great difficulties of traversing these sometimes remote paths in times of appalling weather they were strictly adhered to. In Brittany, rough tracks were made from the outlying farms to the villages so that people might go to the church on Sunday or visit their dead in the graveyard. In the course of time, proper roads were constructed and the old tracks were used only for funeral processions. It was considered sacrilege to conduct the dead by any other way than that by which their ancestors had gone before them, and it was considered bad form for any landlord to prevent a funeral passing by the sacred route.

English funeral paths have ghostly legends attached to them. The Lych Way on Dartmoor was used to bear the dead for burial at Lydford until 1260, and legend holds that ghostly trains of mourners could sometimes be seen walking along it. In a similar fashion the White Stile Ghost is said to haunt a stile, which was once used to rest the coffin, on the funeral path between Carharrack to Gwennap church in Cornwall. Supernatural encounters are also reported on the corpse road from Arndale to Beetham church in Cumbria where fairy folk could be seen on the Fairy Steps, a rock-cut flight of steps on a funeral path (see Directory: The Fairy Steps). Tales such as these may conceal the route of a forgotten corpse road or funeral path where the tradition is long dead and the path no longer remains.

Other beliefs held that a corpse way should cross water on its route, either a stream or a river, sometimes a ford, to ensure that the soul of the deceased would be prevented from returning home after burial. It was believed that spirits could not cross water. In the numerous examples so far collected and published in *The Ley Hunter* since 1992, funeral paths invariably cross over at least one stream. Although it is probable that a funeral path is almost certain to cross over a stream at some point, the folk belief lends a plausible significance to this common feature.

A study by Gabrielle Hawkes and Tom Henderson-Smith in the westernmost tip of Cornwall revealed a number of examples of church paths criss-crossing the Penwith landscape. These paths cross the fields from remote villages and hamlets to the nearest parish church and are often punctuated by old stone stiles between the fields and occasionally by an ancient stone cross. They are usually straight, which will be of interest to ley hunters, and had a ritual significance in the lives of local people who would walk them on their way to church for christenings and funerals. Regular funeral processions took place between Bosullow and Madron between which there is a straight route, taking in sections of footpath and passing the Neolithic dolmen of Lanyon Quoit (see Directory: A Churchway Ley).

Dutch, and some German, examples of death roads have been shown to be dead straight and this may relate to the folk belief that spirits have a preference for straight travel. This is certainly the case for German *Geistewege* or ghost roads. A similar 'ghostly' line is said to link Brailes Hill in Warwickshire with Bredon Hill in Worcestershire (both crowned with earthworks and mounds) over a distance of 23 miles! A right of way was claimed over Brailes Hill because the dead of Brailes were taken to be buried by that path. While this may be a folk memory of some ancient sacred way, or even a spirit route, it is highly unlikely that anyone would have been carried to burial over such a distance (see Directory: Pathway to the Sun). In *Folklore in Shakespeare Land* (1930) J. Harvey Bloom refers to three Warwickshire church roads which used to run from Fulready, Thornhill and Upper Ettington to 'the old church by the hall, long since disused, *in a perfectly straight line*' (my italics). My own recent investigations have been unable to trace these paths.

Hawkes and Henderson-Smith, writing in *The Ley Hunter*, relate the reminiscences of a life-long inhabitant of St Just in Cornwall, who recalled that there were definite paths and routes from out-of-the-way places which were the straightest, most direct way to carry the coffin up to the church or cemetery. These paths were known as coffin lines.

Straight or crooked?

Folklore references rarely describe the exact nature of the funeral paths they mention, apart from one or two notable examples, and it is often impossible to establish whether or not paths were straight, unless some trace still remains on the ground. Ulrich Magin, writing in *The Ley Hunter* in 1993, recounts the folk beliefs of the Württemberg area of Germany in which there is a brief mention of *Totenwege*, or death roads, but no mention of their straightness or otherwise. However, Magin eventually found further references to German death roads which went by the names of *Leichenweg* (corpse road), *Notweg*, *Kirchweg* (church road) and *Helweg* (road to Hell or Hel's road). There were a number of rules that had to be adhered to in the choice of route. These resulted from the belief in the straight movement of ghosts as expressed in the ghost roads, and included prohibiting the blocking of a death road. A woman who had blocked a death road was condemned to haunt it after she died. Sometimes the cortège had to use the same road that the deceased used to use to go to church. This would appease the spirit of the deceased, as it would allow an easy journey home. However, the emphasis was placed on detour, not directness, which suggests that there was a hidden danger in such a journey. The road was believed to take magical characteristics from the dead and could become haunted; the road had to deviate to hinder the spirit's return. In Hesse, for example, it was traditionally the church road that was taken by funerals and not the shortest route. But the detour may ultimately be based on the fear of ghosts and the ill luck, pestilence and death they may bring, as evidenced by the avoidance of passing over fertile land. It was also sometimes necessary to cross water on route to the church in an attempt to prevent the spirit of the deceased from returning, as we have already seen.

These beliefs may be the foundation of the numerous traditions already discussed that necessitate carrying a coffin three times around the churchyard before entering or perambulating an old stone or cross. As late as the 17th century in England most country people believed in the reality of apparitions, the existence of fairies and stories of witches. Fairies are particularly ancient in origin and may represent a real memory of contact with Otherworld entities. These spirits manifested themselves as dancing children frisking in the air, sky-borne black dogs and the aforementioned corpse candles. Fear of these beings was rife and all manner of protective measures were undertaken to ensure human safety. In a similar fashion, the souls of the deceased were considered to be equally dangerous if they were allowed to roam freely, and many precautions were taken in the days following a death to ensure that the disembodied soul would not return to haunt its earthly home.

The question of whether a death road should be straight

or not is by no means clear. Either way, the spirit dimension is well established, as was the belief that the spirits of the dead have a preference for travelling in straight lines. As a result some death roads are straight and others actively avoid straightness by taking a winding, if not a circuitous route (as opposed to simply meandering). Ghost roads, on the other hand, which are invariably invisible, are straight.

One particular type of ritual or symbolic pathway which might add weight to the argument that spirits prefer to travel in straight lines, is that of the maze or labyrinth. The classic labyrinth is a unicursal winding path that twists and turns on itself in a series of coils to reach the centre. Where labyrinths exist in a Christian context they were used by penitents to make a symbolic journey to God. A famous example is the mosaic pavement labyrinth at Chartres Cathedral. Hundreds of stone-built labyrinths exist on the shores of the Baltic Sea, dating from at least the Middle Ages. Folklore records that superstitious Baltic fishermen would enter and walk the labyrinth before setting out to sea, in the belief that trolls and dangerous sprites would become ensnared in the maze and not follow them to sea.

Similar concepts can be found in northern European lore where devices such as 'spirit traps' were used to protect property against evil spirits. Spirit traps consisted of red thread looped around a copper circle in a radial pattern and were set up on pathways between a house and a cemetery to disrupt the passage of sprites (see also Plate 11).

While there are examples of straight funeral paths in Britain, many recently explored examples show variations. Often the general line of the route is straight although the path itself winds around this general alignment, incorporating many straight sections within it. It is possible that if the path was originally intended to be straight, it may have subtly changed its course over the centuries due to deviations to avoid waterlogged stretches, resulting in a wavy line. The enclosure of agricultural land might well explain the odd dog-legs found in the course of the path where field walls and boundaries were laid across the original track. It is an interesting point that in later years Watkins himself conceded that the old straight track could deviate in this way, although he remained adamant that the marker points along its route were always in alignment.

A prime example of this type of path is the funeral path known as Burial Lane in Worcestershire (see Directory: Burial Lane), which runs due south from a hilltop just outside the tiny hamlet of Ham Green, next to a disused chapel. The metalled road becomes a bridle-way, which descends towards Feckenham in a roughly straight line in the direction of the church. At the southern end the path takes a curious curved course to cross the river at Feckenham before joining a section of metalled road into the village and past the churchyard. Other traditional funeral paths take a more convoluted route but incorporate dead straight sections. Such a path runs from Coleford in the Forest of Dean in Gloucestershire to the church at Newlands, the cathedral of the Forest, and I traced and walked this path from near the centre of Coleford along a straight footpath between suburban houses and gardens, across sections of straight track over open fields and through woods to a road crossing and a series of steps. A dead straight section of cobbled track rises to a high point and field boundary before turning sharp left to descend via a paved hollow way into the village of Newlands, ending at the lych gate in the churchyard wall. A straight path then runs from the gate to the church. Another example, preserved in name as Church Path and signposted as such, was shown to me by Gerald Frawley (see Plate 6). It runs from Gotherington to Bishop's Cleeve in Gloucestershire (see Directory: Church Path).

Craig Wetherhill, writing in *The Ley Hunter*, describes a classic Cornish coffin line known as the Zennor Churchway, which is still traceable along its ten-mile course from St Ives to Pendeen. It crosses continuous patterns of small stone-walled fields and is marked by dozens of 18th and 19th century stone stiles. From the 9th century the route was marked by round-headed stone crosses, but only a few remain today. The track is also marked by field names such as Churchway, Way Field and Road Field. The earlier Cornish field name *Furrywidden is vorr an gwidn* means 'the white way'. The name churchway may be a misnomer as the old track avoids the three parish churches it passes by as much as 200 metres. In addition, only one stile on the route is equipped as a coffin rest. Why then, asks Wetherhill, are there waymark crosses? Were they signposts for the spirits of the dead? These crosses are older than any of the churches on the route by at least two centuries and may indicate that the path is significantly older too. Perhaps the church builders avoided placing their churches on or near the path. Such caution was not expressed by the Methodists in the 18th and 19th centuries, who built chapels directly on its path in several places. While not dead straight by any means, the Zennor Churchway follows a linear route with the type of minor deviations noted elsewhere.

Another type of funeral path, noted by researcher Phil Quinn, follows a roughly clockwise circuit, in spite of easier and more direct routes being available. One such path can be followed in the parish of Hawkesbury in South Gloucestershire (see Directory: The Soul's Journey). The dead were once carried from the deep combe of Kilcot, up to the top of the Cotswold ridge where the coffin was rested on a long barrow before they continued south-west down to Hawkesbury church. After the burial the funeral party made its way home, not by the route they had come, but by one which completed a grand circuit adding over a mile to their journey. This custom may reflect the belief, suggested earlier, that the spirit of the deceased would not be able to follow the funeral party home. Funeral parties carrying their dead from Oldmixon to Bleadon church in the Mendips, followed a similarly convoluted route. Here a short and direct route was avoided in favour of an alternative route in a straight line sighted on Hutton church before turning sharp right, southwards up through a steep gully to the summit of Bleadon Hill. From here the party headed south-west down another steep gully to the church. Why, asks Quinn, choose a tiring and tortuous clockwise route when a shorter anti-clockwise one existed? Perhaps the landowner's fear that a funeral party could establish a right of way by passing over private land ensured that there was only one available route. However Quinn suggests that this pattern is too widespread for that argument to hold up.

To add to the confusion over what type of path was the norm, Quinn notes another funeral path at Hawkesbury in South Gloucestershire, of the linear type. It runs from Hillesley, two miles from Hawkesbury (see Directory: The Soul's Journey). The path shares part of the route used by Kilcot funeral parties.

The old straight track revisited

Although Watkins gave it only scant attention, the tradition of the church path was cited by several members of the Straight Track Club during their written ruminations on the nature and origins of the old straight track. In Portfolio 14 (1931) Major F.C. Tyler mentions a good example of a church path at Ashington in Sussex where an old right of way leads across fields from the Manor House, past the Rectory, to the church, a hundred yards to the east of and running parallel to the main road from London to the coast. In response Guy Liddell cites the example of Hatch Beauchamp at Taunton in Somerset. The church there is hidden behind the Manor House and is only approachable by paths and a separate carriageway through the park. Rights of way across the fields to the church also exist.

Barbara Carbonell writes that the name 'church path' referred to rights of way across fields that were used by people going to church from outlying parts of a parish. She mentions one in particular, Church Path at Bow in Devon, which crosses water meadows a quarter of a mile from the church, and which was maintained by the church wardens until recent times. She also notes another, four miles away, known as Churchway, leading from three farms at the extreme end of the parish to the main road leading to the church. She noted the tradition, in Devon, that carrying a corpse along a path renders that path 'a right of way' for ever. She goes on to describe how a friend was approached by her tenant farmer to ask her permission to carry the corpse of a dead relative to the church across one of her fields in order to avoid a long and tiresome drive through the lanes. Her friend was warned by her bailiff that to grant permission would establish the route as a right of way. Despite the fact that this custom is not enforceable under English law it was considered difficult to prevent the locals from exercising this questionable right after the corpse had been carried over her land and she had to refuse permission.

Post-war ley hunting had all but ignored this tradition, preferring to concentrate more on the esoteric nature of energy lines, but by the late 1980s interest had been revived and it was only a matter of time before Watkins's leys came under renewed scrutiny by ley hunters. A famous Watkins ley was re-examined by veteran ley hunter, Paul Devereux. Discussed in some detail in *The Old Straight Track*, the Sutton Walls ley in Herefordshire links Wellington church, Marden church, the Iron Age hill fort of Sutton Walls and a churchyard cross at Sutton St Nicholas church (see Directory: Sutton Walls Ley). The ley actually passes through a visible 'notch' on the edge of Sutton Walls ramparts, and an outlying mound. From this point the spire of Marden church and the tower of Wellington church can be seen in clear alignment. A year after finding this alignment Watkins was approached by the owner of Sutton Walls who told him that ploughing had revealed an ancient track as a dark mark in the field, running up to the mound at the edge of the camp. This old track (Devereux suggests that it might be a medieval spirit way) which when projected to the south-east would have passed not through Sutton St Nicholas church, but through its burial ground, marked by a cross.

Another Watkins ley through Llanthony Abbey in the Black Mountains on the Welsh border, has an ancient 'hollow way' aligning between the abbey and a 'notch' on the hilltop horizon, and the course of the alignment beyond the abbey coincides with curious linear markings on the hillside beyond. This has yet to be satisfactorily explained. The most prominent of these lines is a roughly paved track which Devereux suggests might be a Welsh corpse road cutting straight across the Black Mountains to Llanthony.

Other researched leys revealed hitherto unrecognised elements. A Somerset ley originally found by Anthony Roberts and published in *The Ley Hunter* in 1971 claimed 17 mark points along a 26-mile long alignment. This would stretch the credulity of the most hardened ley hunter, but the most convincing section of this line is a path running through Monk's Ford. This ancient straight track is directly in line with a clearly defined track up the side of a hill about a mile away. Devereux identifies this track as a corpse way used by the monks at Glastonbury to carry coffins on a two-mile journey between Henton church, through Yarley Cross to Wookey. Roberts also found the 'diamond stone' where the coffins were rested on their journey. A mixed-marker ley at Saintbury, near Broadway in the Cotswolds, incorporates a section of documented corpse road in its alignment. Coffins were once rested at the cross before being carried along the road leading up to St Nicholas' church (see Directory: Saintbury Ley).

There is good reason for thinking that some of Watkins's leys may well be remnants of the type of medieval spirit paths we have been examining in this chapter. Devereux suggests that Watkins's leys were a combination of these ghostly features in the landscape, a few genuine prehistoric alignments, and plenty of simple chance alignments. He goes on to say that these spirit ways may have been a medieval development of an idea that had an earlier form in the Neolithic cursus – a type of linear earthwork which usually linked or was aligned on burial mounds. Although difficult to prove, it is possible that the cursus earthwork, besides being a sacred enclosure, may have marked a processional way between long barrows connected with the rites of the passage of the dead. Perhaps they were the Neolithic equivalent of the ceremonial funeral path, which may have been accessible at certain specific points along the length of the cursus, perhaps where it changed direction, as it does several times along the six-mile Dorset cursus on Cranborne Chase.

Major Tyler, writing in Portfolio 11 of the Straight Track Club refers to J. H. Hutton's *Assam megaliths* which records the tradition of erecting alignments of menhirs along a path. Usually these megaliths line the paths that approach a village or some other frequented place. They appear to be associated with the souls of the dead, since the cult of the dead is associated with the paths by which the soul leaves and returns to its earthly habitation. Offerings for the dead are placed along paths in the direction from which the village originally came and in the Ao tribe the dead themselves are exposed along the paths.

The Christian spirit path

It would be premature to suggest that the medieval death road is the sole explanation for leys, as many straight landscape alignments clearly predate that period, but it is certainly a prime candidate for many of the types of alignments involving ancient churches that Alfred Watkins noted when he made his discovery 75 years ago. This explanation may apply to short alignments in Britain, Ireland and continental Europe, where the traditions of the death road and ghost path have survived. But not every Watkinsian ley is a death road and not every corpse path is a ley. The sacred path takes many forms, sometimes straightness is important, other times it is not, but the unifying factor seems to be the spirit element and the characteristics of spirit travel.

The early Christian missionaries who encountered the spirit beliefs and spirit geography of pagan natives branded them as evil. The normal practice was therefore to exorcise the dwelling places of pagan spirits. Although the early churches were raised on the sites of former pagan worship, the ghosts of haunted churchyards are not those of Christian spirits but of demons and apparitions that inhabited burial places centuries before the missionaries arrived.

Ulrich Magin's researches into German ghost roads have led him to examine the ways in which Christian missionaries in Germany went about subduing pagan practices in the early days of the Church. It is well documented that pagan shrines and holy places were often destroyed by the Church or adapted to its own purposes by attaching a saint's name to them or incorporating them into churches and other Christian structures. Another method, albeit previously unnoticed, was the inclusion of pagan sites into Christian sacred alignments. In Germany, in the 10th and 11th centuries, there was a deliberate practice of laying out towns to a sacred geometric scheme. In this replanning, a cathedral was built at the town centre, which was then surrounded with four smaller churches to form a giant imaginary cross covering the whole city. The four branches were engineered to mark the four points of the compass with the cathedral axis oriented east–west, as is the Christian custom. Sometimes the alignments between the four churches and the cathedral were invisible, other times they were marked by roads. In Speyer, for instance, a road extends from the cathedral, along its axis, and forms the city's main street and ceremonial way, the Maximilianstrasse (see Directory: Speyer Cathedral Ley).

This geometric pattern must have been considered important as it was also used to overlay existing cities, which were completely rearranged to accommodate these church lines. Magin suggests that perhaps pagan sites were incorporated into these Christian alignments in order to exorcise them. He gives a convincing example that links ancient and modern sites with burial places, boundaries and folklore – a classic Watkinsian mix.

The *langer Stein* (or long stone) stands 3.7m high at Saulsheim near Alzey, and is a typical example of a Bronze Age menhir. Local legend says another holed stone, called *des Teufels Suppenschüssel* (the Devil's soup bowl) once stood in front of it, which may have been the base for a medieval wooden cross. The *langer Stein* has been Christianised by the carving of a niche in its side which once held a statue. Folklore records its location as the result of it having been thrown by the Devil from Donnersberg. Since 1724 the stone marked the *thing* or court of justice for local people and it also marked a parish boundary. A gallows once stood by the menhir and several ancient roads including a main Roman highway crossed at it. Magin suggests that the Christian Church must have considered the stone to be of great pagan significance as it chose to build the mountain church of Udenheim close by. This church stands on the site of a Roman temple whose altar was incorporated into its walls and is linked to the *langer Stein* by a straight path along the axis of the church. Along this path lie Roman and pre-Roman burial grounds. Archaeologists consider the alignment to be deliberate.

Magin speculates that the association of Christian lines with pagan sites, as well as with gallows sites and pagan legends, led to the belief, in some parts of Germany at least, in straight ghost roads. Whatever its possible origins in the distant past, the tradition of straight roads for spirits became culturally associated with the Christian creation of church lines and alignments to pagan sites. The folk concept of the spirit path, opines Magin, is the result of a long struggle between pagan and Christian ideas. Straightness was sacred to both and Magin suggests that the Christian church lines came from the idea of reserving a special straight road for the passage of spirits, one set apart from the profane and winding roads of country folk. He sees superstition leading to the belief that these old alignments were ghost roads, for evil spirits only, despite their original intention of enhancing the power of a cathedral and symbolising the spread of Christian holy spirit and influence throughout a town or city.

The unravelling of the straight line enigma is a difficult one, crossing as it does cultural and temporal boundaries. In all the cases discussed in the preceding chapters the one constant unifying feature of all our examples is the spirit element, and it is from this that everything else follows. From the demotion of sacred pathways into utilitarian roads, the recording of celestial solar and lunar alignments via stone rows and megalithic monuments, the scratching of dead straight lines across miles of South American desert, the encountering of ghostly apparitions on lonely European trackways to the bizarre rules applied to the transportation of corpses to burial, we counter humankind's lingering obsession with the straight line. None of these alone is a ley, but a ley can be all of these things. By his simple discovery of the old straight track in the Herefordshire countryside, an eccentric Edwardian gentleman has opened up a 75-year-old quest for the meaning of the archaic landscape line, a quest which continues to puzzle and fascinate each new generation of ley hunters. The feature of ley hunting lies hidden away in obscure chapters of folklore books and local history studies. Tantalising snippets of information, references to funeral routes, ghost tales and traditional customs can lead the enthusiastic ley hunter to the discovery of an ancient track or pathway still surviving in the countryside. By map reading and by walking the old routes and observing the surrounding landscape it is still possible to reconstruct the old spirit paths and rediscover the real 'ley of the land'.

CHAPTER 8
HOW TO HUNT
LEY LINES

'Ley hunting gives a new zest to field rambles,
and the knowledge of the straight ley provides
new eyes to an eager observer.'
Alfred Watkins, *Early British Trackways*

Alfred Watkins laid down meticulous rules for ley hunters
in his books, and provided advice to would-be ley
hunters. These can be a useful tool for the modern ley
hunter to emphasise the pitfalls and blind alleys that await
the enthusiastic novice, and also because these early methods may prove helpful. Remember one thing though: leave
your dowsing rods at home – this is ley hunting in the true
Watkinsian tradition and must be treated as an activity incorporating reference research, mapwork and fieldwork.

Watkins was convinced of the existence of prehistoric
alignments in the landscape, and his advice to ley hunters
derives from his conviction of the absolute precision of
the ancient surveyors. Fieldwork is essential: 'It is surprising how many mounds, ancient stones and earthworks are to
be found which are not marked, even on the large-scale
maps', he says. This observation still holds true today, and
is particularly relevant since modern updated OS maps show
even fewer prehistoric features than they did in Watkins's
time.

What to look for

Watkins maintained that mark points, standing stones and artificial mounds were laid out by prehistoric surveyors, ley-men or dodmen, as he called them, to mark the old straight tracks for wayfarers and merchants, and he gave the following points to look out for on the map, listed in order of importance.

Ancient mounds, whether called tumulus, tump, barrow, cairn or any other name

These were the most important markers, Watkins claimed. From their summits the surveyors and later travellers could spot the next marker point and make for it, eventually creating the tracks that run between them. This class of mark point could include Neolithic long barrows, trapezoidal mounds of earth, chalk or stone, which sometimes contained stone passages and chambers in which the bones of the dead were interred. Similarly, he included Bronze Age round barrows. These were usually smaller than long barrows and often contained only one burial crouched at the centre. Both types of mounds were frequently sited on the 'false crests' of hills such that they would be visible in silhouette against the sky when viewed from the valleys below and thus would make excellent sighting points. These can often be found on the Ordnance Survey map marked '*tumulus*' or '*tumuli*'.

Ancient unworked stones – *not* those marked 'boundary stone'

Another class of marker is the single standing stone. Standing stones would have played a similar role to the later milestone, brought to England by the Romans, in that they marked the route of the old straight track. Standing stones can vary in height from the foot-high unnamed and unworked mark stone often found lying beside the road, to

the colossal 22-feet tall Devil's Arrows in Yorkshire. Watkins
suggested that such stones were placed at the crossing points
of two or more tracks. Furthermore, he suggested that the
crossroads mark stone might well have evolved into the
Christian wayside cross which would have ensured the survival of the ley marker to the present day.

Moats and islands in ponds and lakelets
Water-sighting points were another Watkins marker. Many
round mounds in Herefordshire had a moat or ditch surrounding them, which probably held water at one time.
Simple ponds, too, were singled out by Watkins. On more
than one occasion his own archaeological excavations under
dried-up ponds revealed old paved tracks which confirmed
the course of his leys. He also suggested that ponds and
moats might have served as easily-spotted sighting points on
the track, where they would have stood out brightly in the
landscape as they reflected the sky above. Many surviving
moats that one finds on maps are more often than not later
constructions designed as defences for isolated farmhouses
and are unlikely to be of any value in ley hunting. They can
usually be detected by their rectangular shapes.

Traditional or holy wells
Watkins always maintained that leys ran between what he
called initial sighting points, that is from one prominent hill
to another, although sometimes they ran from a holy well to
a hill or vice versa. All the markers between these initial
points would invariably be artificial and laid out by the
ancient surveyors. Sometimes holy wells can be found close
to or in the precincts of ancient churches, which may suggest that the siting of the church may have been influenced
by the location of an older holy shrine.

Beacon points and camps

Watkins found that many camps (now more frequently referred to as hill forts) were constructed at the crossings of two or more tracks. To be more precise, he said they were built in the angles formed by the alignments. Time and again, Watkins observed that his leys ran along the banks and ditches of hill forts rather than through their centres. Hill forts date from the Iron Age and are usually found on high ground, often on the summits of prominent hills, and can vary in complexity and size. Essentially they are areas of flat ground defined by banks and ditches which have been identified by archaeologists as having some defensive purpose (hence the use of the word 'fort'). Watkins claimed that older mounds were incorporated into the later camps thus preserving the earlier ley markers.

Beacon fires on prominent hilltop locations were once traditionally lit on Midsummer's Day and Beltane. This practice continued until a century ago in Herefordshire and was adopted by Watkins as a possible survival of ancient sighting practices involved with the laying out and maintenance of the old straight track. Although the fires may no longer have been lit, their memory is preserved in names such as Bell or Beltane Hill, May Hill and Midsummer Hill. Watkins found beacon pits on several hills carrying that tradition; the fire or smoke would have provided the ley men and travellers with a clear sighting point along the track, he surmised.

Crossroads with place names, ancient wayside crosses and fords

There were several other types of landscape feature, which Watkins adopted as confirmation points along his leys. These included old crossroads, fords, hollow ways (sunken roads with high banks on either side) and fragments of straight tracks and roads which followed the exact course of a ley. Although the roads now radiating from crossroads do not preserve the course of the old straight tracks, the crossing points still preserve the old route, he surmised. These were often marked by mark stones and later wayside crosses. Again, ancient place names often confirm the validity of the mark point. Crossroads were once considered special places and treated with reverence. They were liminal spaces – a no-man's land – the sites of gibbets and gallows and where suicides were often buried. Watkins claimed that traces of old straight tracks could be seen at fords where they crossed rivers and streams. Notches on the ridges of hills where the old hollow ways crossed over were prominent sighting points too.

Churches of ancient foundation and hermitages

The most contentious sighting points are churches and castles. Clearly these are not prehistoric, but their recurring frequency on Watkins's leys suggests some kind of connection. The class of churches which were acceptable as ley points were pre-Reformation structures dating from Anglo-Saxon foundations, through Norman and early Gothic to the time of Henry VIII. Drawing on documented sources and folk memory, Watkins suggested that ancient churches were invariably built on sites of earlier pagan sanctity. A Papal directive from AD 601 clearly instructs Christian missionaries to Britain to acquire pagan sites of worship for the new religion to ease the transition from paganism to Christianity. Examples of this practice can be found all over Britain: the ruined church at Knowlton in Dorset erected at the centre of a Neolithic henge (a circular enclosure surrounded by a bank and ditch); the church at Rudston in Yorkshire built adjacent to the tallest standing stone in England; and the church at Alfriston in Sussex (the Cathedral of the Downs), placed astride an ancient mound. There are many more. Not all churches, though, can be said to be so sited, and it is an interesting observation that Watkins noted many examples of sections of old straight trackways and leys passing through churchyards and burial grounds rather than the churches themselves.

Ancient castles and old 'castle' place names

Norman castles are another problematic sighting point. As they frequently fell on his leys, Watkins felt obliged to find an explanation for this. Norman castles of the classic 'motte and bailey' type consisted of a central stone keep (the bailey) built on the top of a tall mound (the motte). Watkins concluded from archaeological evidence, which indicated a construction earlier than 1066, that the Norman administrators had chosen to build their keeps on existing and prehistoric mounds where they found them. Sometimes they enlarged the original mounds. Again, the original ley markers were preserved by their later use.

Watkins suggests ringing each of these features on the map so that they are clearly visible. Then, stick a pin into the exact location of a primary marker point, such as a standing stone, stone circle or mound, and place a straight edge against it, swinging it around to see if three other ringed points (or two and a stretch of straight road or track) can be found to align. Draw a thin pencil line through the points and then check for further confirmation points along its course. The line can be transferred to an adjoining map by careful alignment of the sheets on a drawing board or large flat table, or by transferring the bearing of the line by use of a protractor and tee-square. Accurate map work like this requires time and effort and many ley hunters confine their searches to single sheets. This can be limiting but necessarily keeps any found alignments to a manageable length, a factor to bear in mind when following the ley in the field. To conform to the Watkins prototype, the ley should consist of at least four marker points and terminate at both ends in a natural hill or mountain peak. Prepare yourself for some disappointment if you are ley hunting in East Anglia!

If you are successful in this first stage, the next thing to do is to walk the ley on the ground. Notwithstanding the difficulties of crossing private land, motorways and rivers, it should be possible to visit each of the ley marker points and to walk part of the alignment. For this it is essential to carry a good compass with which to orientate yourself in the field.

Perhaps the most exciting aspect of ley hunting in the Watkins tradition is the discovery of a straight track or road on the course of a ley. It is often difficult to find locations where three marker points can actually be seen in alignment, but very satisfying when you do. The second best 'confirmation' is a fragment of straight track, or road on the course of a ley, especially when it can be seen to align with a marker point such as a church spire or prominent hill or hill fort.

Watkins found several examples of old straight trackways running up the sides of hills or as hollow linear depressions across unploughed meadows and orchards. Often the old trackways can be seen at the right times of the year when variations in the vegetation show up as ghostly shadows of a former path. Watkins was without the benefit of aerial photography in his day, and many linear and other archaeological features have been discovered by this method in recent decades. Among them, the cursus monuments, most of which have been discovered by this method, have been shown to contain numerous alignments to prehistoric barrows, standing stones and ancient churches. In addition he included underground tracks, that is remnants of old trackways now buried under centuries of accumulated soil. Watkins himself discovered several in Hereford during the excavation works for new sewers, and recent archaeological excavations at Hereford Cathedral, prior to the erection of the new building to house the famous Mappa Mundi in 1995 revealed a well made cobbled road precisely in the location Watkins had predicted whilst working on alignments in the city 70 years earlier.

Straight roads

Watkins urges the ley hunter to keep his or her eyes open when cycling or driving along a straight stretch of road, and to look out for any hill point or mound, church or castle on a bank, which is not only straight in front, but remains fixed in the same position as you travel. In some areas of the country, map-work can reveal stretches of straight road that align accurately on ancient churches that might indicate the presence of a Watkins-type ley; I located three such road alignments in Gloucestershire.

There is a remarkable alignment near the village of Withington, some six and a half miles south-east of Cheltenham. Driving towards Withington on the A436 between Andoversford and Kilkenny, on top of the Cotswolds, the road suddenly straightens out and runs across country in a dead straight line. At the point where the road dips into the village and on a direct line of sight is the squat tower of St Michael's and All Angels church. The straight section of road is approximately two miles long. Curiously, it diverges from the alignment (out of sight from the upper and middle sections of the road) and skirts around the churchyard. Prompted by this discovery I attempted to project this alignment in both directions to see if any other sighting points or markers remained on the ground. Heading northwards the line passes over Cleeve Hill, one of the prominent peaks on the Cotswold escarpment, but unfortunately the line misses the banks of an Iron Age hill fort and the curious ring earthwork on the lower slopes of the hill. It does, however, pass through the summit of the hill (now marked by a trig point bollard). In the other direction the line passes through St Michael's church, close to the summit of Chedworth Beacon and on to St Mary's church at Barnsley. Not a classic ley by Watkins's standards, but a curiosity, a fragment of old straight track running on a line drawn between two prominent hills.

The Romans were very active in the Cotswolds and the existence of any straight sections of road not marked on the map as 'Roman road' or 'Course of Roman road' are probably Roman in origin or possibly the result of the enclosures. There are the remains of two Roman villas close by. If the road were Roman in origin it is a strange coincidence that St Michael's was built on the line of the road. Perhaps the church occupies an earlier sacred site? This is where ley hunting takes you into the library in search of local history and archaeology.

In isolation this occurrence is merely interesting, but it is not the only example I have found in the area. The B-road between Northleach and Aldsworth in Gloucestershire, winds its way through the village of Eastington and skirts the edge of Lodge Park in a straight line of no obvious significance (though probably the result of the enclosures). The road then takes a sharp left and then bends on to a dead straight section on high ground that points directly to the tower of St Bartholomew's church on the brow of a hill in Aldsworth. The straight section of road is about a mile long, but abruptly ends at a T-junction shortly before the village. The road then drops into a hollow and down into the village. It does not go to the church. Like the Withington line this deviation in the course of the road is not visible from the upper reaches of the road. Projecting this alignment on the map in both directions found it passing through nothing of significance apart from a crossroads on the old Salt Way some seven and a half miles away from Alsworth and, to the south-east, through the edge of Dean Camp in a suitably Watkinsian manner (through the edge of the ramparts), a mile from the church.

Another alignment, which will be familiar to regular users of Ermine Street, the stretch of Roman road between Gloucester and Cirencester, is that of the road and the tower of Cirencester's church. Between Birdlip and Cirencester it consists of several straight sections of road linked together. The final stretch south of Daglingworth is aligned on the church tower, a prominent landmark in the low-lying land around Cirencester. Within the town itself, Tower Street aligns to the church tower though it does not run to the church. It also lies adjacent to the site of the Roman forum. As in the previous two examples, Ermine Street diverges from the alignment at the point where the road begins to descend the Cotswolds. Outside the town again the Fosse Way is also aligned to the church tower from the west. The church tower would have been a convenient sighting point for the Roman surveyors in the laying out of these two major routes, however it wasn't there when the roads were built. The church, dedicated to St John the Baptist, is often refereed to as the Cathedral of the Cotswolds and is the largest parish church in the county apart from Tewkesbury Abbey and larger than three of England's cathedrals. The earliest surviving building dates from the Norman period.

Similar patterns of road and church alignment can be found on a map, but it is only by visiting the sites that the true nature of the alignments can be appreciated. The examples given above are probably Roman roads; the roads around Cirencester certainly are, but the survival of the others is curious in the present-day random system of winding lanes. At the very least they can give a flavour of what Watkins must have envisaged when he discovered the ley system and provide a great opportunity for a quick ley hunt.

The difficulties of ley hunting

An important aspect of field observation is that of intervisibility of sites. In short distance leys, such as those between standing stones, the ability to see the next marker stone from your point of observation is a good indication that the alignment was deliberate. John Michell used this method in his study of leys in West Penwith, Cornwall. It was also by this method that several marker stones not shown on the map were discovered. What appears to be a convincing ley on the map can often be a great disappointment if the next site is not visible.

Of course, the changing landscape in Britain has obliterated most of the evidence for leys. The old stones have either been taken for road building or walling, the ponds have been filled and prehistoric mounds flattened by the plough; it is a tough job now to follow any promising alignment. The novice would be advised to start with an already established ley to get an idea of what to expect to see when attempting to follow an alignment. A point to bear in mind when starting a map search for new leys is that some parts of the country are more likely to yield up promising alignments than others. The kinds of mark points that Watkins describes are found in greater numbers in the western regions of Britain, whilst standing stones and megalithic monuments are rare in eastern areas where the geology doesn't provide suitable building stone. Built up urban areas are also a problem as many of the original features have been obliterated by modern urban development. Some areas simply have no suitable remaining mark points at all. Like a true hunter, prepare for disappointment or failure. This makes the discovery of an alignment, and especially a visual one, all the more satisfying.

Watkins claims that this is detective rather than surveying work. As he says in *The Old Straight Track*: '. . . if the evidence were plentiful and easy to find the ley system would have been discovered long ago . . . ancient tracks and roads have disappeared (and most of the barrows and mark stones) wherever the plough touches, and that bits to be found are few and far between.'

Since its inception in the 1920s ley hunting has taken on many guises. It was a great source of amusement for the leisured classes in the 1930s and, as Watkins rightly observed, added an extra dimension to a Sunday ramble. That urge to get out into the country lay behind the motives of later ley hunters, who even armed with dowsing rods were discovering the landscape and its history. Watkins has been much maligned over the intervening years, however, and ley hunting has fallen out of favour with those interested in the ancient sites and landscapes of Britain. The rapidly changing face of much of the countryside, the spread of development and the building of more and more roads has made the simple pleasure of walking along the old straight tracks of the countryside more difficult than it has ever been.

Watkins was aware of the difficulty in defining exactly what constitutes a ley and was only able to give his personal opinion. A ley, he said, is an alignment of sites, but does not infer that a track was established exactly along a line, or even at all. The ley was an optical line used as a guide for a track. There is less evidence for tracks along some leys, and here Watkins mentioned, in particular, alignments of hill forts, which he referred to as 'camp alignments'. In some cases, he stated, it is possible that there never was a track along them. He went on to say that these trackless alignments are nevertheless leys and that the mark points on them never deviate from the straight line. A church or mark point is never 'near' an alignment. The track may have gone to one side of the mark point but the ley never did.

However, the recent developments in ley hunting have called into question some of Watkins's original conclusions about the nature of leys, and this has led to an entirely new branch of field investigation that takes its lead from some of Watkins's observations regarding old tracks. As previously discussed, many of Watkins's old straight tracks may well have been medieval in origin. These tracks were used for traditional ceremonies and activities associated with death and burial. Fresh clues to the mystery of ley lines can be found by following these old routes and observing their idiosyncratic features and tracing their history and archaeology.

Ley hunting today

Modern ley hunters are more likely to start their search for ancient trackways in the local reference library. The local studies collection is a good starting point, though these days there are many fine studies of local village histories which often contain obscure references to old funeral paths and church paths. Infrequently, if ever, will you find references to leys – so don't look for them. Once you have tracked down a reference, a good place to start is the local County Records Office, where it is usually possible to consult the old tithe maps which were drawn up at the time of the Enclosure Acts. Sometimes the names of the old tracks are preserved as well as significant features that may have since disappeared. Also try the local Victoria County History as you may find a reference or two there.

Armed with this information, it is time to consult the Ordnance Survey map. The older versions of these are preferable as they often contain a wealth of detail missing from the modern maps and will show areas of the countryside which are now developed, and old footpaths that have disappeared. Search out local secondhand bookstores as you can often pick up old maps very cheaply; try to trace the old funeral paths or corpse ways. This can often be a frustrating task as the old route will not be named and there may be several possible footpath routes between the locations you have found in the books. In the absence of any written record of the route go for the most direct. This will invariably run from a village without a church, or with a recent church, to the village which once held the burial right. Once you have found a likely contender, get out into the field.

The Ley Hunter has been publishing reports of ley hunting activity for a few years now and it is apparent that no two tracks are the same. Some useful hints can be gleaned from them. You will also see from the examples given in the Directory of Ley Lines that visiting the sites, talking to locals and checking the documented history and archaeology of the sites can lead to some interesting discoveries. One thing is clear: landscape lines come in many shapes and forms and have their origins in historic times as well as the distant past, and as we have seen, some may even cross-over and contain elements from different periods. The types of old trackways, alignments and leys that can be found are many and varied. Not all of them are classic Watkinsian leys, but they indicate a preference to construct religious and ceremonial tracks and sight lines in a linear fashion, which may have their roots in the ancient beliefs in the spirits of dead ancestors and the manner in which they were thought to travel. These can loosely be grouped under the following headings and examples of each type of landscape line can be found in the Directory at the back of this book.

Watkinsian leys

The classic ley is usually first found on the map, but should be followed up by field and archive research to verify the significance, if any, of the alignment.

Astronomical alignments

This is a somewhat specialist area, principally due to the complexity of some of the mathematical calculations required to establish the rising and setting points of the sun and moon at various latitudes and elevations. Simple observation at ancient sites can give an indication of a significant alignment, but reference to nautical almanacs and the map are necessary to verify any suspicions. A useful tip is that the formulae for the calculation of the azimuths of the rising (or setting) sun can be found in John Wood's *Sun Moon and Standing Stones*. This type of alignment searching is not for the casual ley hunter, however. Going to visit the sites and experiencing the well-known astronomical alignments is a worthwhile activity in itself.

Corpse roads, funeral paths and coffin ways

Corpse roads are often found in the mountainous northern parts of England and Scotland. They are usually several miles long and follow arduous and sometimes dangerous courses over hills and mountains. They are rarely straight.

Funeral paths are numerous in the Midlands of England and references to them can be found in local libraries, on old maps and in the many books now available on village histories. Collect as much information as you can before setting out. Unlike the conventional Watkins ley, most of these paths can still be walked. They are usually preserved as public rights of way, although over the intervening few hundred years parts of the original routes have sometimes been moved making it difficult to check sight lines and straightness. Always get permission before following any track that is not marked as a right of way.

Medieval church alignments

These are often preserved routes or alignments of varying ages which link prominent religious structures, usually churches, with important secular sites. Classic examples can be found in the old centres of Oxford, Bristol, London and York amongst others. Also look for astronomical alignments of such paths and tracks.

Prehistoric linear features

Those with an interest in archaeology can often find references and articles describing discoveries of ancient trackways, ceremonial roads and linear features connected with burial mounds, and earthen enclosures such as henges in the archaeological press. Popular journals such as *Current Archaeology, British Archaeology* and *Archaeology Ireland* are good sources of potential material.

Spirit paths and ghost roads

Ghost sightings in isolation along stretches of old straight track or road are interesting but not particularly significant. However, detailed local research can reveal the incidence of hauntings, folk tales of ghostly journeys and paranormal events along stretches of old tracks and roads, and when these are found in combination with known ancient tracks and standing stones, mounds and holy wells they can lead to some interesting discoveries.

Tips for the would-be ley hunter

From the above examples it can be seen that modern ley hunting encompasses a wide range of disciplines; the modern antiquarian needs to be archaeologist, local historian, archivist, walker, mathematician and surveyor. The range of possibilities for the ley hunter are wide enough to accommodate any enthusiasm, be it for megalithic sites, walking in spectacular or forgotten landscapes or simply retreading the steps of Alfred Watkins.

Walking the old paths can be a revelation. Old references to a paved funeral path can be confirmed by finding the old cobbles underfoot. Some old routes are named, while some sections may have been unused for years. Take plenty of photographs, note any features not shown on the map which may be significant, check the local history collections at the library and talk to any local people you might meet, but be wary of mischievous locals who can mislead you. Finally, keep a look out for other sighting points, which may have been part of an original ley before it was adopted for a funeral route.

When researching in thinly populated areas with a wealth of prehistoric features, look out for alignments to significant horizon features or other visible standing stones and mounds. These may indicate astronomical alignments, another class of line that Watkins recognised. Armed with a map and compass it is possible to check these alignments for any astronomical significance.

For a guide to Watkins's own brand of ley hunting, the best book to refer to is his own *The Old Straight Track*. This is still in print and has the lost charm of times gone forever. It is the best guide to leys in the Welsh border region and many of Watkins's famous leys can still be traced and walked. Watkins's language is sometimes laboured but he writes with great enthusiasm and it is difficult not to be drawn into his lost world. His later *Ley Hunter's Manual* condenses the essentials of early ley hunting into a concise handbook, but is no longer in print. For a practical, down-to-earth guide to the intricacies of map work and Watkinsian ley hunting, the best available book is *The New Ley Hunter's Guide* by Paul Devereux. This contains practical tips for working with OS maps and for accurately transferring plotted leys from one OS sheet to another. It also has a section of leys that Devereux and Ian Thompson first published in *The Ley Hunter's Companion* (now out of print) with additional information that reinterprets the alignments in the light of more recent theories as to the nature of ley lines.

There are numerous books covering the energy line school of thought that touch on leys, but all are necessarily subjective accounts of the author's experiences and not the best practical guides. The most level-headed of the bunch is *Ley Lines – Their Nature and Properties* by the late J. Havelock

Fidler. In it the author manages to fuse his own dowsing experiments with map work and a little archaeoastronomy in an attempt to interpret and understand the numerous alignments of standing stones, though only in a remote part of western Scotland.

The important thing to remember about ley hunting is that it is a participation sport. In order to understand the nature of these alignments and old tracks you have to get out and walk them. Simply reading about leys will get you no closer to understanding them. Walking is an essential element as the view from the ground can show you much more than the map. Keep your eyes open. In a landscape as heavily farmed and developed as Britain the remains of the old straight tracks and ancient pathways are few and far between, but sufficient tantalising clues remain to make ley hunting an exciting and rewarding pastime.

Get hunting!

ENDWORD
WHERE DO I GO
FROM HERE?

By the late 1980s, the straight track had for many become just a succession of false trails, a waste of time and effort. Alfred Watkins had always disliked the idea of believing anything that could not properly be explained. However, his theory became associated with crackpots and fanatics, and has still not received the recognition it deserves, although the work of Paul Devereux has been instrumental in prompting the need for re-assessment.

Today, ley hunters are perhaps more circumspect than their colleagues in the Straight Track Club decades before. The exigencies of modern life and the destruction of huge tracts of evidence by successive agricultural policies, vandalism, town planing and heritage bodies has made ley hunting difficult, complicated and, in some areas, plain impossible. Other evidence, however, is available, and certainly the attitude of the archaeological establishment has moved from intolerance to cautious attentiveness. A great deal of examination and assessment has taken place and, 'unhampered by other theories' (not least because no one theory is dominant), it is again possible to continue the work of Watkins, his colleagues in the Straight Track Club, and a handful of other pioneers since. Most importantly, there is a new environmental awareness, which at least makes it difficult for officialdom to dismantle sites and areas of great archaic and archaeological value. Today's ley hunter is by nature somewhere between a conservationist and an environmental warrior.

During my time as editor of *The Ley Hunter* I have been asked on numerous occasions by people from as far afield as Australia and the United States, as well as from all over Britain and Europe, if I can supply them with a map of the ley lines in their area. Each time I have to say no. Such maps do not exist. There are, of course, local studies for some areas, and there are one or two books that describe the more famous alignments, but as there are as many different interpretations of leys as there are ley hunters it is very difficult to make an objective assessment of any of them let alone catalogue and map them.

This book is an attempt to clarify the confusion over the interpretation of Watkins's original vision and to place ley hunting back on a firm footing. I don't have all the answers and there is much more work to be done, but this book sets out to define the parameters of ley hunting (and they are pretty wide) in order to give the would-by ley hunter the tools needed to do the job. The future of the subject rests in the hands of those who want to get out in the field to find and walk the old trackways themselves. Learn about your immediate vicinity and its history; take a hike and keep your eyes open – there's a lot to see and discover.

Where do I go from here, you may ask. This is straightforward: get involved. I invite all interested readers of this book to register with The Society of Ley Hunters. If there is sufficient interest we will contact all correspondents with a view to putting like-minded individuals in touch across Britain and Europe for the exchange of ideas and discoveries, and to build up a directory and maps of leys for future researchers. This is an ongoing project where participation is open for all.

Write to The Society of Ley Hunters at:

The Society of Ley Hunters
PO Box 1634, Hassocks BN6 8BZ
Or e-mail at: clement@pavilion.co.uk

We also have a web site where you can access archive material, check on the latest research and news, find book reviews and obtain books on leys and related subjects from our mail order book service. You can also post messages in our guest book and contact other ley hunters worldwide. The web site can be accessed at: www.leyhunter.com

A DIRECTORY OF
LEY LINES

This is a collection of alignments of the types described in this book. It includes some of the leys discovered by Alfred Watkins, some of a similar nature that have been found by modern ley hunters inspired by Watkins's vision, astronomical alignments, acknowledged prehistoric alignments of sites and stones, sacred pathways, funeral routes, death routes and spirit paths.

It is not an exhaustive list, that would be an impossible task, but it is designed to give a flavour of the many types of alignments that have at one time or another come under the heading of 'ley lines'. From this list it is clear that there is no one single type of landscape line that can definitively be called a ley, but these examples demonstrate mankind's continual obsession with the straight line or path in the landscape.

I have selected examples that take in some of the more famous prehistoric sites in Britain. I have also chosen examples from areas which are easily accessible and some from wilder places for those who enjoy combining their interest in megalithic sites with walking in open countryside. In addition I have included a number of examples from Ireland, Malta and mainland Europe which show that ley hunting is not confined to Britain.

The list is a random one with the type of alignment classified by an identifying icon at the top of the page. The 1:50,000 Ordnance Survey sheet numbers are given for the British and Irish examples. I hope the following will encourage the curious to visit and experience these tracks and places and perhaps even to take up ley hunting for themselves.

KEY

 This symbol denotes a ley discovered or written about by Alfred Watkins himself.

 The image of the chalk hill figure of the Long Man of Wilmington in Sussex was adopted by Watkins as a representation of the 'dodman', the ancient surveyor of the leys. It denotes a Watkins-type alignment discovered by others.

 The solar symbol denotes an alignment of astronomical significance, either solar or lunar.

 The symbol of death denotes a funeral path, death road or coffin path.

 A medieval church alignment.

 A relatively short alignment of prehistoric remains that form a complete monument or construction, such as a stone row or avenue.

 A spirit path or ghost road.

A BELGIAN ALIGNMENT
A megalithic ley near Wéris

This is an alignment of contemporary mega-lithic structures, acknowledged by Belgian archaeologists as deliberate and planned. Two miles out of the town of Erezée at Bouchaimont at Oppagne stands a group of three menhirs, which were re-erected in 1906 (**1**). The tallest stone is 8ft tall. The line is at right angles to the alignment which leads northwards to the half-buried *allée-couverte* (or passage grave) near Wènin (**2**). The next site on the line is a 12ft menhir (**3**) built into a wall at the side of the road. This stone had been toppled and buried but was restored in 1947. Over half a mile further on the line passes over the Dolmen de Wéris (**4**), a major dolmen over 36ft long with a huge capstone. Both dolmens on the line are orientated upon it. Further along the line to the north are the remains of fallen menhirs (**5**), broken up at the end of the 19th century. These may have formed another line like the Oppagne group marking the end of the alignment.

Three menhirs at Oppagne. Based on an etching by John Palmer.

A BELTANE LEY
Aubigny au Bac, France

The ley was first noted by Eugene Zimmer and was published in *The Ley Hunter* no. 129 in 1988.

The village of Aubigny au Bac is situated on the River Sensee near Douai in northern France. The ley runs roughly south-east to north-west through a chapel outside Aubigny au Bac (**1**), the village church (**2**), a prehistoric menhir at Brunemont (**3**), and church at Arleux (**4**), ending at St Martin's church at Bellone (**5**).

Zimmer calculates the bearing of this ley to lie within those given for the setting sun on the Celtic Quarter Day of Beltane, the spring festival. Viewed from the menhir, the sun sets on Beltane on the horizon at the foot of the church at Bellone (**6**).

The dedication of the church gives a clue to the validity of the alignments. St Martin was the Merovingian's most revered saint and his dedication was frequently used for the Christianisation of former pagan sites of worship. The church itself is small and built in a Romanesque style, confirming its antiquity. Further, the name Bellone is derived from Belenus, the Celtic sun god, whose feast day is none other than Beltane (1 May), all of which suggests that St Martin's was built on a prehistoric site probably as old as the menhir at Brunemont.

The alignment has been preserved and extended during the medieval period by the establishment of other churches and chapels.

BLACKWARDINE LEY

AW The first discovered ley

(OS 1:50,000 Landranger Sheet 149)

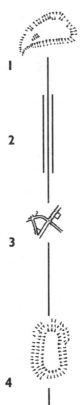

1

2

3

4

5

On the opening page of *Early British Trackways* Alfred Watkins describes the moment of his discovery of the ley system. A visit to Blackwardine, now preserved only in the name of a cattery, led him to consult the map and notice a line running from Croft Ambrey Iron Age hill fort (**1**), over Risbury Camp (**4**) and ending at a high point near Stretton Grandison where he thought a Roman station once stood (**5**).

Standing at Blackwardine today it is difficult to see what triggered Watkins's imagination. The high ground at Stretton Grandison is crossed by the line of a Roman road, now preserved as a farm track, and the site of Watkins's Roman station is hidden in trees. Risbury camp, though prominent on the map, is virtually invisible at ground level as it is thickly planted with trees. At Croft Ambrey hill fort, though, it is possible to get a flavour of what Watkins must have surmised in 1922. From this lofty position can be seen every prominent hill for miles. It takes little imagination to appreciate how this might have been a crossroads for the prehistoric traveller with only the next hilltop as a way marker.

From the top of Croft Ambrey a track descends through the modern forestry plantation and becomes a metalled road called Croft Lane. This winds its way around the line of the ley and for about a half mile lies directly on the line (**2**). I also found what may have been a mark stone (**3**) at the Blackwardine crossroads exactly on the ley.

BOYNE VALLEY LEYS
Newgrange, Knowth and Dowth, Ireland
(OS of Ireland 1:50,000 Sheet 50)

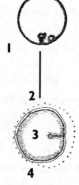

The Boyne valley in County Meath, Ireland, is dominated by three enormous Neolithic chambered mounds: Newgrange (**3**), Knowth (**1**) and Dowth (**5**). Newgrange contains a passage and central chamber which is illuminated by the midwinter rising sun, Knowth has two passages aligned directly east and west, and Dowth has two passages, one of which is aligned directly with Newgrange. The Dowth alignment is augmented by two of the standing stones in the circle (**2, 4**) surrounding Newgrange mound which lie exactly on the alignment.

In a similar fashion, two more of the stones in the circle (**6, 7**) fall on a line drawn through the perfunctorily named Mound 6 (**8**), an outlying burial mound, and Newgrange and Knowth.

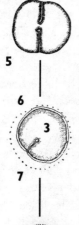

Both leys cross at a stone in the central chamber of Newgrange, which archaeologists have designated R21. From this stone lines run to each of the surrounding stones in the circle pointing to astronomical and topographical features. In addition, R21 aligns with the engraved kerb stone at the entrance to Newgrange and a kerb stone at the rear. Both are marked with a straight vertical groove which are aligned with the passage and the midwinter sunrise.

There is little doubt that these alignments are deliberate and that the circle surrounding Newgrange was probably erected prior to the building of the mound.

BURIAL LANE
A funeral path at Feckenham, Worcestershire

(OS 1:50,000 Landranger Sheet 150)

A fine example of a burial path still exists at Feckenham in Worcestershire, approximately six miles west of Redditch; the inhabitants of the outlying hamlets of Cruise Hill and Ham Green once had to convey their dead two miles for burial at Feckenham.

From Cruise Hill, the beginning of the route is marked by a derelict chapel on the bend of the road (**1**) and a modern street sign reads 'Burial Lane'. The route passes a few houses before deteriorating into a track that descends through a dark tunnel of trees towards Feckenham. The path is preserved as a bridleway and maintains a good width all the way; it is also quite straight and keeps a sightline on the church. There is a slight dog-leg in the path half-way along where the field boundaries have been altered, but it then continues relatively straight again. A small but very old iron gate (**2**) stands in the middle of the path.

The path then sweeps around in an arc to avoid the river before resuming a line on the church tower. Shortly before the road, two other paths meet the burial path which then crosses the river by a footbridge (**3**) passes the old mill race and joins a metalled road leading up to the church (**4**).

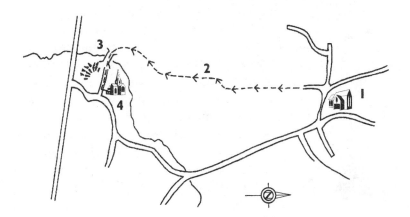

CERNE ABBAS LEY
A Dorset holy hill alignment
(OS 1:50,000 Landranger Sheet 194)

7

6

5

4

3

2

1

Landscape lines are many and varied, and not all are examples of the same type of track or sight line. Frequently, alignments and sometimes tracks that lie upon them can be found linking sacred places to high hills and mountains. Paul Devereux has identified a class of ley which he calls a 'holy hill alignment'; the Cerne Abbas ley may be an example of this pattern.

Running approximately north–south for seven miles, this ley starts at St Lawrence's church (**1**) at Holwell in Dorset, a 15th century church with Saxon origins. It then passes through a tumulus (**2**), a prehistoric settlement site (**3**) and on to Giant's Hill where it passes over the Trendle (**4**). This is a rectangular earthen banked enclosure that lies a short distance above the head of the famous chalk hill figure of the Cerne Abbas Giant. The Trendle is an Iron Age construction and was later used for traditional May Day celebrations.

The next ley point is the ruined abbey at Cerne Abbas (**5**); the first abbey was founded in the 9th century by St Augustine who is reputed to have had a vision at the site. The line passes through the nearby wishing well (**6**) with its links to fertility, healing and divination, and terminates at the 13th century St Mary's Church (**7**) in the village.

A CHURCHWAY LEY
A Cornish spirit path
(OS 1:50,000 Landranger Sheet 203)

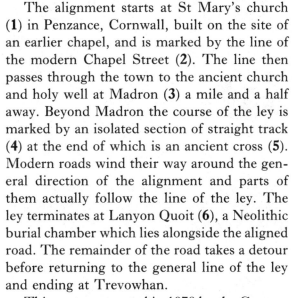

This alignment is a classic and controversial mixed-marker ley in the Watkins fashion. It is also a church path and coffin line. Paul Devereux suggests that this line was made up from markers of varying ages along what he described as a 'myth line' with its origins in the human imagination.

The alignment starts at St Mary's church (**1**) in Penzance, Cornwall, built on the site of an earlier chapel, and is marked by the line of the modern Chapel Street (**2**). The line then passes through the town to the ancient church and holy well at Madron (**3**) a mile and a half away. Beyond Madron the course of the ley is marked by an isolated section of straight track (**4**) at the end of which is an ancient cross (**5**). Modern roads wind their way around the general direction of the alignment and parts of them actually follow the line of the ley. The ley terminates at Lanyon Quoit (**6**), a Neolithic burial chamber which lies alongside the aligned road. The remainder of the road takes a detour before returning to the general line of the ley and ending at Trevowhan.

This route was noted in 1978 by the German author Hans Steuerwald whose bizarre theory held that Atlantis was located at Penzance! Steuerwald believed that Ulysses had landed at Portheras Bay in the Bristol Channel. In the *Odyssey*, Ulysses is led to the town of the Phaiacians (Penzance) along a path that leads past holy wells to the city walls, and Steuerwald found what he believed to be the path along the very same track that Devereux was to find.

CHURCH PATH
A funeral path between Gotherington and Bishop's Cleeve, Gloucestershire
(OS 1:50,000 Landranger Sheet 163)

In the Middle Ages Gotherington did not have its own church and the villagers were obliged to attend St Michael's church in Bishop's Cleeve for baptisms, marriages and burials. The path taken by the villagers is still traceable across the fields, running from Shutter Lane (**1**). This path was never a bridle-way. Beyond the village the line of the path has been diverted to run through a mobile home park, though the original and straight route can still be discerned in a bracken-choked swathe running alongside a field boundary (**2**). Beyond, the path can be seen preserved in an unploughed section of field proceeding in a straight line in the general direction of St Michael's church (**3**) whose tower is visible on the horizon. The final part of the path is now lost under modern development (**4**) though older maps still trace its course.

The original purpose of this track is preserved in the old hand-painted sign fixed to a cottage wall at the start of the route which reads 'Church Walk' (**5**).

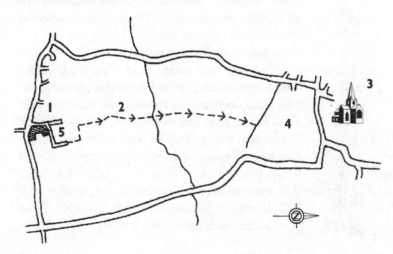

COLDRUM LEY
A statistical argument in Kent
(OS 1:50,000 Landranger Sheet 188)

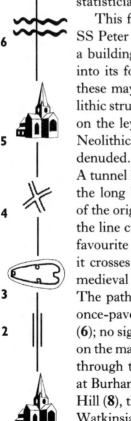

In 1980, ley hunters were keen to prove that leys were more than the chance alignments of points on a map. This particular ley came under close scrutiny by the statisticians and did not pass their tests. However, Paul Devereux, who first noted the ley, pointed out that field-work and archive research can reveal evidence to back up the deliberate nature of alignments that simple mapwork cannot, overriding the statistician's use of maps alone.

This four and a half mile alignment starts at SS Peter and Paul church (**1**) at Trosley, Kent, a building of Saxon origin with large stones set into its foundations. It has been suggested that these may be the remains of a destroyed mega-lithic structure. The mean axis of the church falls on the ley, and the line can be projected to the Neolithic Coldrum long barrow (**3**), now partly denuded. Its chamber stones are clearly visible. A tunnel legend (**2**) connects Trosley church and the long barrow, which may be a folk memory of the original alignment. Three miles further on the line cuts through an old track crossing (**4**) (a favourite Watkins marker point) and beyond that it crosses All Saints (**5**) at Snodland, where the medieval Pilgrim's Way skirts the churchyard. The path used to cross the River Medway at a once-paved ford that lies on the line of the ley (**6**); no sign of the ford can be found today, either on the map or on the ground. The ley then passes through the redundant church of St Mary's (**7**) at Burham Court before terminating at Blue Bell Hill (**8**), the original initial sighting point, in true Watkinsian fashion.

DEVIL'S ARROWS LEYS
Two Yorkshire bullseyes
(OS 1:50,000 Landranger Sheet 99)

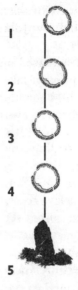

The Devil's Arrows stand in fields outside Boroughbridge in North Yorkshire, perilously close to the A1 motorway. The three megaliths form a straggling line and range from 18 to $22^{1}/_{2}$ ft in height. Though the stones themselves do not constitute an alignment, two lines can be drawn through the stones that align with nearby henges and mounds.

The first alignment was noted by Norrie Ward and connects the three Bronze Age Thornborough henges (**1, 2, 3**). These massive, ditched and banked earthen rings are each about 800ft in diameter. A Neolithic ceremonial avenue or cursus has been discovered passing under the middle henge. A mile in length, the cursus ditches are 100ft apart, though nothing can now be seen from the ground. The ley clips the edges of two northernmost rings and bisects the third. It also bisects a fourth henge at Nunwick (**4**), though this is now much ploughed out, and the central Devil's Arrow (**5**). Subjected to a statistical analysis by Bob Forrest, this line was found to be a beyond chance alignment.

The second line, noted by Paul Devereux and Ian Thompson, links the central and southernmost Arrows (**6, 7**) and can be projected northwards to clip the edge of Cana henge (**8**), another earthen ring in this unmatched concentration of sacred sites, and a tumulus at Low Barn (**9**). Many Bronze Age burial mounds cluster around the henges. The ley terminates on the north-western edge of Hutton Moor henge (**10**).

A DUTCH LEY
Steeplechasing in medieval Holland

This is an alignment of secular and Christian sites in south Holland, first noted by John Palmer in *The Ley Hunter* no. 104.

The ley starts at a windmill (**1**) situated on an island in the middle of Kagerplassen lake. The oldest mills were built on the high ground or on a dyke. The ley then passes through Huis de Warmond castle (**2**), rebuilt in the 13th–17th centuries, and on to the ruined Warmond church (**3**). A church is known to have been here in 1063; the later Gothic church was destroyed in 1573 leaving only the tower and the cemetery. Below the church there are extensive underground tunnels, one of which leads off in the direction of the ley towards a circular moat (**4**) where the 13th-century castle of Teylingen and later a Cistercian religious house once stood.

The line then passes through Groene Kerkje near Oegstgeest (*geest* meaning spirit) and another windmill (**5**) before terminating at the site of Rÿnsburg church and monastery (**6**). This last building was torn down in 1573. There have been several churches on this site, the earliest, a chapel, being constructed in AD 100. A cloister was established in 1133 and a church built in 1170. The site was excavated in 1949 and the ley accurately passes through the churchyard and the outline of the building.

The ley is approximately four and a half miles long.

THE FAIRY STEPS
A Cumbrian corpse way
(OS 1:50,000 Landranger Sheet 97)

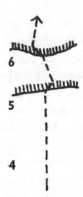

Supernatural encounters are reported on the corpse road from Arndale (**1**) to Beetham church in Cumbria. The path which consists of a series of straight sections follows a dead straight course (**4**) from Hazelslack Tower Farm (**2**), named after the ruined stone fortress (**3**) that still stands on the farm, to the Fairy Steps (**6**).

At Whin Scar, the straight corpse road is forced to make a series of dog-leg turns as it ascends the scar in two flights of stone steps (**5, 6**). The second flight is known locally as the Fairy Steps (**6**) and it is an impossibly steep rock-cut stairway at the bottom of a very narrow gully. The idea that pall-bearers could manoeuvre a coffin up this cleft is hard to believe.

Tradition has it that the fairies will grant your wish if you can skip up the Fairy Steps without touching the sides. I have attempted this feat without success. In places the cleft is as narrow as a foot at shoulder height. Those with the second sight are believed to be able to witness the fairy folk skipping up the stairway.

The approach to the Fairy Steps at Whin Scar, Cumbria.

HOLY HILLS IN
NORTHERN GAUL
French leys and
archaeoastronomy

In the region of Douai in northern France, the Belgian ley researcher Eugene Zimmer has identified a number of classic 'holy hill' alignments which are both astronomical and topographical in nature. Douai is situated 100km south-east of Calais and the hills in question have churches at their summits, one of them in the village of Oisy-le-Verger (**1**).

Four megalithic sites (three menhirs and one dolmen) and two holy hills lie close together on the borders of the River Sensee. One of the hills has a pronounced shape and is crowned by the chapel of Notre Dame de Montaigu (**2**).

Zimmer has noticed that in many areas where such 'holy hill' alignments can be found, the alignments of sites usually point towards the local summits, but always in solar, and sometimes lunar, directions.

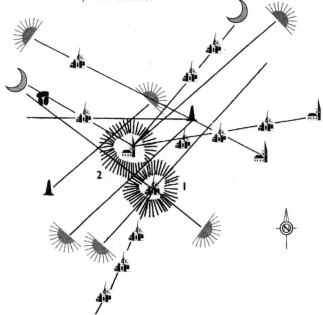

*Holy hill alignments around Voisy-le-Verger
identified by Eugene Zimmer.*

ISLE OF ARRAN
A line of circles on Machrie Moor
(OS 1:50,000 Landranger Sheet 69)

Machrie Moor, on the Isle of Arran, is a deserted plain two miles wide and bounded by hills, that contains the remains of what must have been a great centre of religion and culture. The remains of numerous hut circles, chambered cairns and stone circles can be found all over the moor, many of which are buried in the peat. The circles vary in size, shape and the types of stone used to construct them.

Dave and Lyn Patrick, writing in *The Ley Hunter* no. 98, described their investigations on Arran and their discovery of a dead straight alignment of features across Machrie Moor and beyond.

On the highest point of the moor are the remains of a hut circle (**1**), from which a ruined chambered tomb (**3**) and another huge hut circle (**6**) can be seen in line. They walked this line and came across another hut circle (**2**), a circular mound (**4**) and a further hut circle (**5**), all falling on the line. The line seemed to terminate in the south-west at another hut circle (**6**) from which all the other sites can be seen.

Towards the north-east the line crosses Machrie Water and terminates on high ground at a mound (**7**).

Another linear feature the Patricks came across was a pair of parallel banks, 80ft wide, running approximately north–south for one and a half miles and aligned with a hut circle. The date of construction of this earthwork is unknown, though archaeologists consider it to be a boundary.

KNOWLTON HENGE LEY
An astronomical alignment
(OS 1:50,000 Landranger Sheet 195)

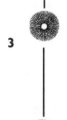

5

4

3

2

I

This short alignment was published in 1914 in a little book entitled *The Green Roads of England* by R. Hippisley-Cox. Before Watkins, others had noted alignments which either pointed to significant topographical features or the rising and setting points of the sun and moon at significant times of the year.

Hippisley-Cox's book is about the ancient ridgeways of England and attempts to trace the routes of our Neolithic ancestors. The concept of leys had yet to come about, but it is likely that published alignments like this played their part in Alfred Watkins's discovery.

The alignments links three tumuli (**1, 2, 3**), probably Bronze Age, and Knowlton henge (**4**), a circular earthwork with an outer bank and inner ditch. The line passes through a break in the outer bank, through the centre of the henge and points in the direction of sunrise (**5**) at the summer solstice (21 June).

The Church considered Knowlton henge significant enough to erect a church within its precincts, and the ruins of this building can still be seen today.

No-one is really sure what henges were used for, as very little in the way of artefacts has ever been found in them. They were probably multifunctional areas where religious and secular activities took place, much in the same way that churches were used in the early years of Christianity.

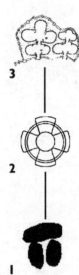

LEYS ON GOZO
Megalithic alignments on the Maltese islands

Malta and its neighbouring Mediterranean island are famous for their prehistoric megalithic temples, and it would appear that some of these were deliberately aligned. In *The Ley Hunter* no. 113, David Olmen described two such alignments on the island of Gozo, with a common origin at Ta' Cenc dolmen (**1**), a complex of megalithic structures, some of which have been compared to megalithic gallery graves in Sardinia and Italy.

A straight line links this site with the Ggantija Temple (**3**), another complex dating from 3800 BC, consisting of two temples within a common boundary wall. Some of the stones are up to 18ft high. The ground plans of both temples have been compared to the squatting 'goddess' figurines that have been found on the island. The site that sits between them is Xewkija church (**2**), with the third largest dome in Christendom. The present church is modern but is built on the site of earlier Christian structures and a large dolmen, last recorded in the 17th century, which was used as the foundations of the church.

The second alignment runs from Ta' Cenc to Tal Qighan (**4**), which consists of two groups of megaliths lying on both sides of the road and may once have been part of a temple. The line ends at Qala menhir (**5**), a 13ft high standing stone which is now surrounded by modern houses.

LINES OF STONES
The menhirs of Carnac
(IGN carte topographique 0821 est)

The most well known of the Breton megalithic sites are the multiple lines of huge standing stones near the village of Carnac in southern Brittany.

The largest group of stone rows are at Kermario. The cromlechs that stood at both ends of the rows are now gone, but a restored passage mound still stands in line with the southernmost stone row. Cromlechs are spacious rings of close-set standing stones whose shapes may have derived from earlier passage graves and were probably used for open air rituals connected with death and burial.

The next largest group, at le Menec, has twelve roughly parallel rows of stones running between two cromlechs. The West cromlech is a huge egg-shaped stone ring and the East cromlech a smaller egg-shaped ring. Many of the original stones are missing, robbed for road building and so on. The stone rows, which have been added to over the centuries, may have marked ritual processional ways or death roads between the funerary sites.

The Kerlescan rows north of Carnac also run to a cromlech. At the western end alongside the cromlech there is a *tertre tumulaire*, a rectangular burial mound, reinforcing the link between death, burial and the rows of stones. Kermario means 'place of the dead' and Kerlescan means 'place of burning', which gives some indication of the activities that once took place at the ends of alignments. The rows at Petit Menec were probably once contiguous with the Kerlescan rows and terminate at a circular structure.

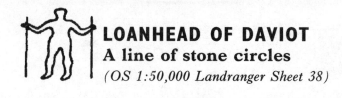

LOANHEAD OF DAVIOT
A line of stone circles
(OS 1:50,000 Landranger Sheet 38)

This is an alignment of three Neolithic recumbent stone circles, so named because of the large recumbent stones that lie at the south-west of the circles. These massive flat-topped boulders are usually flanked on either side by upright stones, all three framing the area of sky and horizon where the midsummer moon sets.

The circle of Loanhead of Daviot is the best preserved of the three aligned rings. The circle in Daviot churchyard was removed in 1820 and all that remains of New Craig is the recumbent, its flankers and a few odd stones now built into a field wall. It can be seen clearly from Loanhead.

At less than a mile long this alignment was probably deliberate.

New Craig as seen from Loanhead of Daviot stone circle. Drawing by Jeff Saward.

LONDON LEYS

Church lines in the capital
(OS: 1:50,000 Landranger Sheet 176)

Watkins did not confine his ley hunting to rural Herefordshire, and church alignments (at least) can be found in Old London.

St Martins-in-the-Fields, St Mary-le-Strand, St Clement Danes (pre-conquest and once held by the Knights Templar) and St Dunstan's, Fleet Street, align to the site of an ancient mound approximately at Arnold's Circus in Shoreditch. This ley is approximately seven and a half miles long and parts of Pall Mall and the Strand fall on the alignment which led Watkins to conclude that the ley had probably been an old trackway. The earliest churches on the present sites date from the 6th to the 13th centuries.

The second alignment links St Paul's, Covent Garden, with The Temple church (a Knights Templar round church), St Bride's, Fleet Street, a church on Ludgate Hill, one near the Guildhall, St Stephen's, Coleman Street, and St Botolph's, Bishopsgate. The Temple church and St Bride's are oriented on the ley.

The third ley links the Temple church (**1**), St Paul's Cathedral (**2**) (build on Ludgate Hill), St Helen's Bishopsgate (**3**) and St Dunstan's, Stepney (**4**). Watkins also claimed that two other churches and the bank site (the site of a former church) fall on the line whilst Devereux and Thompson claimed that this line could be extended to St Clement Dane's (**5**). The inclusion of St Paul's on this alignment suggests that it may be another example of a holy hill alignment. St Paul's, St Helen's and St Dunstan's all orient closely on the same angle as the ley.

MAY HILL LEY
Headless men and phantom coaches
(OS 1:50,000 Landranger Sheet 163)

A good indication of the authenticity of a ley is a visual confirmation on the ground. The main part of this particularly striking example is a little over four miles long and starts at the Giant's Stone long barrow (**1**) near Bisley in Gloucestershire. No visible traces of this Neolithic burial mound are left today, but the original stones must have been quite large for the locals to have associated them with giants. Local folklore records that headless people have appeared and suddenly disappeared on the ancient trackway that passes close by.

The next marker is Wittantree (**2**), a high point now marked by an OS trigonometry stone. The Saxon Wittantree Hundred moot place once stood nearby and may have got its name from a sacred tree. A Roman grave was also found at this place.

From the trig point, the rest of the ley can be clearly seen. The line passes over the escarpment to descend and pass over Bull's Cross (**3**), an ancient meeting of tracks and roads made famous by Laurie Lee in *Cider with Rosie*. Tales still survive of a phantom coach seen careering through the crossroads in the dead of night. The spire of Painswick church (**4**) can be seen on the line standing out against the dome of May Hill on the other side of the River Severn. St Mary's is one of only two churches in England where the ancient ceremony of 'clipping' the church still survives. On the feast day of St Mary parishioners join hands around the church in a human chain. May Hill (**5**) completes the ley as a classic initial point.

MERRIVALE LINES
Dartmoor stone rows
(OS 1:50,000 Landranger Sheet 191)

Dartmoor in Devon is littered with the megalithic remains of our Neolithic ancestors. One particular type of monument that occurs in abundance on the moor is the stone row, and two good examples can be found not far from the main road at Merrivale. Two parallel double rows (596ft and 865ft long) can be seen. The first has its east end blocked by a standing stone, the other has a small cairn with a stone circle around it about half-way along its length. There is also a single row with a cairn at one end.

Sir Norman Lockyer proposed an astronomical purpose for these stone rows, suggesting they were used as processional roads, or *via sacra*, but he was incorrect in his calculations. Others have suggested that the spacing of the stones revealed distinct units of measure employed in their layout, that they were part of a larger landscape geometric scheme or that they were avenues or processional paths of the Druids. None of these ideas have much credence. What is certain though is that the lines, rows and avenues are formal approaches to venerated stone circles and burial places. Prehistorian Aubrey Burl has noted that avenues with widely spaced rows led to stone circles, double rows led to round cairns or barrows (burial places) and all had a ritual significance. One might ask the purpose of the blocking stones. They would certainly block the way of anyone wishing to walk between the rows. Were they perhaps a symbolic blocking to the passage of the spirits of the dead ancestors buried at the ends of the rows?

THE 'OLD ROAD' AT WICK
A funeral path between Wick and Pershore, Worcestershire
(OS 1:50,000 Landgranger Sheet 150)

In the Middle Ages Pershore Abbey held the burial rights to the surrounding villages and local people were obliged to carry their dead for burial to Pershore. The funeral path from the village of Wick (**1**) was noted by Wayne Perkins in *The Ley Hunter* no. 130. It consists of two straight sections with a change of direction at a bridge over the River Avon (**2**). The old road west out of the village can still be traced by existing public footpaths. Beyond the river the unsurfaced path can be seen worn across a field and pointing directly at the tower of Pershore Abbey (**5**) to the north. Further on, the route is preserved as a hollow way (**3**) between two fields and blocked by a wicket gate and a stile. In Pershore itself the route becomes Church Street (**4**), but the original use of the road is preserved in its old name, Lice Street ('lice' or 'lyce' being the Saxon word for corpse).

The route is not without its ghostly connections either. Pershore Abbey was once host to a screaming phantom and monks have been seen silently passing through the streets of Wick. A local eccentric by the name of Benwell Hudson, a monk at Pershore was known for his insistence on travelling to Pershore on the 'old road', even if it meant clambering over fences and going through hedges. The old road was abandoned after 1700.

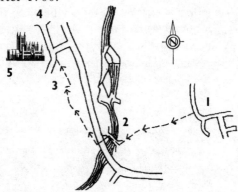

OLD SARUM LEY
A classic alignment
(OS 1:50,000 Landranger Sheet 184)

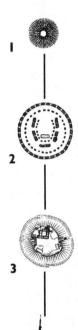

This is probably the most famous ley in England. First noted by Sir Norman Lockyer in 1906, this classic alignment was discovered independently by Alfred Watkins. An examination of the map reveals that lines drawn between Grovelly Castle, Old Sarum (**3**) and Stonehenge (**2**) form a precise equilateral triangle with sides six miles in length.

Old Sarum is an impressive circular earthwork enclosure dating from the Iron Age, and was reoccupied in turn by the Romans, the Saxons and, finally, in medieval times, where it became a town complete with castle keep and cathedral.

If the line between Stonehenge and Old Sarum is extended south it passes directly through Salisbury Cathedral (**4**) to clip the edge of the Iron Age hill fort of Clearbury Ring (**5**) and, if the angle of the line is slightly altered, ends at another hill fort, Frankenbury Camp (**6**). In *The Ley Hunter's Companion*, Devereux and Thompson noted that the altered line, if extended northwards, passes through a tumulus on Durrington Down (**1**). This impressive alignment is dramatically visible from the ramparts of Old Sarum. Salisbury Cathedral spire, the tallest in England, can be seen against the silhouette of Clearbury Ring; legend has it that when it was decided to move the old cathedral from the Iron Age earthwork at Old Sarum, an arrow was shot from the ramparts and where it landed was to be the site of the new cathedral.

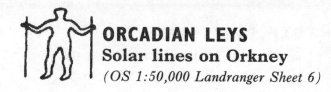

ORCADIAN LEYS
Solar lines on Orkney
(OS 1:50,000 Landranger Sheet 6)

Orkney is famous for its fine collection of megalithic monuments: The Ring of Brodgar henge and circle of stones (7), the Stones of Stennes (5) and the vast chambered mound of Maes Howe (1). The latter has its passage oriented directly to the point on the horizon where the midwinter sun sets (3). To reinforce this alignment a standing stone was erected over 900 yards away at Barnhouse (2) as a foresight.

This and other solar alignments were first noted by Magnus Spence, an Orcadian schoolmaster, in 1894. A line linking the Watchstone, an 18ft high monolith (4) and Maes Howe points to the equinox sunrise. These alignments can be clearly seen both on the map and on the ground. Alignments upon the Ring of Brodgar point to hills where fires were once lit to mark the Celtic festivals of Beltane (1 May) (8) and Samhain (Nov 1) (6). These alignments can be clearly seen both on the map and on the ground.

Alexander Thom, who surveyed the sites in the 1970s, found alignments to the moon from the Ring of Brodgar.

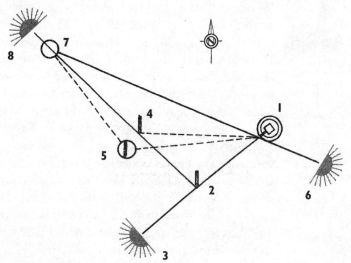

A diagram of the alignments around Stennes identified by Magnus Spence.

OXFORD CITY LEYS
Medieval church alignments
(OS 1:50,000 Landranger Sheet 164)

In *The Old Straight Track*, Alfred Watkins draws attention to the alignments of churches in some of Britain's old cities, notably Hereford, Bristol and Oxford.

At Oxford, two church leys cross at St Martin's Carfax in the centre of the city and in fact define the two main axes of Oxford, Queen Street/Carfax/High Street and Magdalen Street/Cornmarket Street/St Aldate Street running approximately north-south and east-west.

The north-south line includes St Giles (**A**), St Mary Magdalen (**B**), St Michael's (**C**), St Martin's Carfax (**D**), St Aldate (**E**), crossing the Thames at 'Oskna Ford', now Folly Bridge (**4**). The east-west links St Peter's in the Castle (**H**) (now demolished), St Martin's Carfax (**D**), All Saints (**G**) and St Mary the Virgin (**F**). St Martin's Carfax lies on the highest part of the old city and was once the assembly point for council, justice and commerce. The streets which follow the courses of these two lines deviate to avoid the churches.

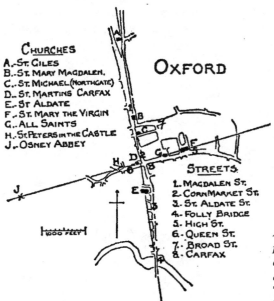

Alfred Watkins's plan of the Oxford church and street alignments from The Old Straight Track.

THE OXFORDSHIRE WAY
A coffin path between Noke and Islip
(OS 1:50,000 Landranger Sheet 164)

The Oxfordshire Way (1) is an official walking route joining together a number of old rights of way across country. As is the case in many parts of the country, old funeral paths are often preserved as public footpaths, though their original functions have long since been forgotten.

A section of coffin path lies on the Oxfordshire Way between the villages of Noke (2) and Islip (3). Part of the parish of Noke was granted to Islip by Edward the Confessor, who was born at Noke in 1004. The parishioners of Noke were thereafter obliged to carry their dead for burial at Islip.

Laurence Main noted this line in *The Ley Hunter* no. 130. It runs in a straight line for much of its route, but not directly between the village churches. Curiously, it follows a line parallel to one drawn between the two buildings keeping to the high ground.

According to Main, if the line is extended to the south-east it hits the site of a former Norman palace at Beckley; north-west it passes through the church at Hampton Gay.

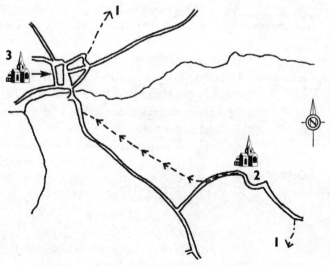

PATHWAY TO THE SUN
Burial road or pilgrim's way?
(OS 1:50,000 Landranger Sheets 150 & 151)

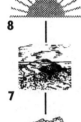

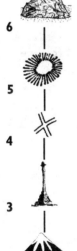

This may be a unique example of the coincidence of a straight landscape line, an astronomical alignment *and* a traceable and documented burial path.

In 1929 J. Harvey Bloom recorded a Warwickshire legend of 'a right of way (that once existed) over Brailes Hill because the dead of Brailes were taken by this path to be buried.' The path was said to run for 23 miles to Bredon Hill in neighbouring Worcestershire. A long way for a funeral!

Brian Hoggard noted an alignment of sites running from Brailes to Bredon Hill which he felt might have been the origin of the burial path legend. It runs due west from Castle Hill (**1**) in Brailes, a flat-topped natural hill that has been reshaped in the past and may have been a Norman castle, over Dover's Hill (**2**), the site of the infamous Cotswold Olympics and the possible site of a turf maze, through a cross (**3**) at Saintbury (see Saintbury Ley), a crossroads at Hinton Cross (**4**), an earthwork at Elmley Castle (**5**), and on to the Banbury Stone (**6**), an elephantine shaped mass of rock at the edge of an Iron Age hill fort on Bredon Hill. Projected westwards the line bisects the Iron Age British Camp (**7**) on the Malvern ridge and marks the equinoctal sunset (**8**).

Alfred Woodward has recorded his researches into an ancient pilgrim's trackway that may be the burial path referred to in the legend. Its route, marked by motor roads and public footpaths, snakes around the course of the alignment passing burial places along its route and skirting the lower slopes of Brailes Hill on its way to Bredon.

RHONDDA CAIRNS LEY
A Welsh astronomical line
(OS 1:50,000 Landranger Sheet 170)

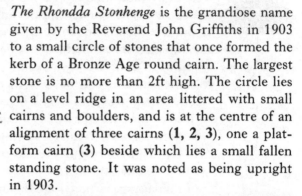

The *Rhondda Stonehenge* is the grandiose name given by the Reverend John Griffiths in 1903 to a small circle of stones that once formed the kerb of a Bronze Age round cairn. The largest stone is no more than 2ft high. The circle lies on a level ridge in an area littered with small cairns and boulders, and is at the centre of an alignment of three cairns (**1, 2, 3**), one a platform cairn (**3**) beside which lies a small fallen standing stone. It was noted as being upright in 1903.

Dewi Bowen investigated this site in 1988 and first noted this astronomical alignment in *The Ley Hunter* no. 111. By observation in the field Bowen was able to confirm that the three cairns of the complex were roughly aligned on the midsummer sun as it set on the horizon (**6**). By transferring the azimuth of the sunset to the map he found that a line drawn from the cairns passed through the Iron Age hill fort of Maendy Camp (**5**). Bowen had earlier dismissed this as a foresight for the solar alignment as it was of a much later date than the Bronze Age cairns and also of some considerable size. However, the line actually passes through the centre of a Bronze Age cairn (**4**) in the middle of the hill fort. This was probably the foresight and must originally have been considerably larger to have been seen from the Rhondda Stonehenge and to have survived the construction of an Iron Age camp around it. The line of the sunset passes through a place called Pen Disgwlfa which means 'the lookout'.

THE ST MICHAEL LINE
The path of the dragon?

The St Michael line is probably the most well-known and celebrated 'alignment' in Britain. It is the one most frequently referred to by the casual observer, but its existence has been hotly disputed in ley hunting circles ever since it was first mentioned by John Michell in *The View Over Atlantis* in 1969.

Its sheer length, from Cornwall to Suffolk, begs the question of its method of construction, as does its somewhat questionable 'straightness'. However, its longevity owes more to its poetic qualities than its accuracy. Most of the sites on the line cluster in the south-west and have a connection with St Michael or St George (traditional dragon slayers) or have some allusion to dragons or serpents.

A line can be traced from St Michael's Mount (**1**) off the coast of Cornwall at Marazion, close to a succession of churches, megalithic sites and places of traditional sanctity. On its way to Avebury it passes close to the Hurlers stone circles on Bodmin Moor (**2**), St Michael's church on the rocky summit of Brentor on the edge of Dartmoor (**3**) (not actually on the alignment), the ruined St Michael's church on top of Burrowbridge Mump in Somerset (**4**), St Michael's church, Otherey Somerset (**5**), the ruined St Michael's church on Glastonbury Tor (**6**), Stoke St Michael church (**7**), Avebury henge in Wiltshire (William Stukeley's serpent temple) (**8**), the church at Ogbourne St George in Wiltshire (**9**) and thence across siteless country to end somewhere near Bury St Edmund's Abbey.

SAINTBURY LEY
A ley and a funeral path combined
(OS 1:50,000 Landranger Sheet 150)

One of the most convincing leys published in *The Ley Hunter's Companion* by Paul Devereux and Ian Thompson is that found at Saintbury in Gloucestershire on the edge of the Cotswolds, near Broadway in Worcestershire. It links sites of different eras with unnerving accuracy and follows a section of straight road (**2**) running from a cross (**1**) and crossroads up towards St Nicholas' church (**3**), over the Cotswold scarp to a Bronze Age round barrow (**4**), through a Neolithic long barrow (**5**), a pagan Saxon cemetery (**6**), and terminating at Seven Wells Farm (**7**), a place locally associated with medieval witchcraft. Whatever one may think of the merits of linking sites of widely differing ages in a straight line, it is now clear that the lower part of this alignment was part of a corpse way. The cross was used to rest the coffin before the arduous climb, along the present road, to the church of St Nicholas.

This ley was subject to a rigorous statistical analysis in the 1970s by mathematician Bob Forrest. The line proved to be 'significant at the 1% level', which means that the alignment was probably deliberate.

This ley, running approximately north–south, shares a marker point at Saintbury cross with an east–west ley running from Brailes in Warwickshire to Bredon Hill in Worcestershire (see Pathway to the Sun).

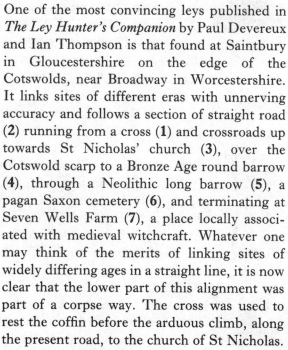

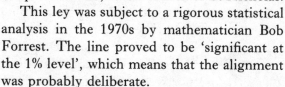

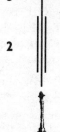

A SCOTTISH ROYAL LEY
Kilmartin Valley, Argyllshire
(OS 1:50,000 Landranger Sheet 55)

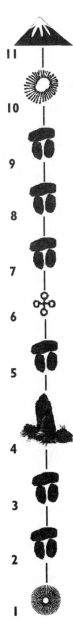

Kilmartin Valley is the home to an extraordinary concentration of prehistoric monuments dating from 4000 to 1200 BC. The dominant feature of the valley is a straight line of burial cairns that follows the contour of the valley.

The first site on this line is an un-named cairn north of Crinian Moss (**1**). A further 280 yards on is the small and denuded Rowanfield cist (**2**) whose axis points along the ley to the next site, Ri Cruin or the King's Circle (**3**). Ri Cruin is a well preserved prehistoric tomb with elements dating from 4000 BC. It is 60ft across and contains three chambers and carved stones. Six hundred yards further on is a 6ft high standing stone (**4**) incised with cup and ring marks. Another 230 yards on is the Nether Largie South chambered cairn (**5**), 130ft in diameter and dating from 3500 BC, the tomb of a king or queen. The next site, a chambered cairn (**6**) was destroyed at the turn of the century. A further 450 yards on is Nether Largie mid-Cairn (**7**), 100ft across and also considered to be a royal tomb. Two hundred yards on is another huge regal tomb, Nether Largie North (**8**), dating from 3000 BC. The final tomb on the line is Glebe Cairn (**9**), once the tallest on the line.

If projected further north the ley passes through Dun na Nighinn (**10**), Fort of the Girls, and terminates at the natural pyramidal peak of Dun Chonnalaich (**11**), the Fort of King Connal's people. Beyond the hill and visible from Ri Cruin is Dun Dubh, the Black Fort where ritual fires were once burned.

SILBURY HILL LEY
An old straight track?
(OS 1:50,000 Landranger Sheet 173)

The area around Avebury in Wiltshire has many prehistoric sites, and many a straight line can be drawn through them on the map. One of the more interesting alignments is that first noted by Paul Devereux in *The Ley Hunter's Companion*. At 13 miles long this might be easy to dismiss if it wasn't for some corroborative evidence that supports both the straight track and spirit path ideas.

The ley runs from Bincknoll Castle (**1**) in the north, a Norman motte and bailey, to an ancient well (**2**) at Broad Hinton, through the church-yard of St Peter's (**3**) at Broad Hinton, via the lych gate, through the western bank of the Neolithic Avebury henge (**4**), on to Silbury Hill (**5**), the largest man-made mound in Europe, of Neolithic origin. Beyond Silbury the line passes through the site of a lost stone circle (**6**), first noted by William Stukeley and surveyed again in 1877, on to Tan Hill (**7**), the site of a former fair, and the crossing of an earthwork ditch (on the line) and the Wansdyke, a massive post-Roman bank and ditch that once served as a boundary. Phantom funerals have been seen at this point. The ley terminates at Marden henge (**8**), the largest henge monument in England at the point where a barrow once stood.

Documentary sources from 1828 mention a 'British track' that used to link Marden and Tan Hill in a straight line. Another track, possibly on the same line, once ran from Beckhampton, south of Avebury, to Tan Hill. So perhaps this is an 'old straight track' and maybe a ghost path too.

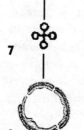

SLIGO FAIRY PASSES
Spirit paths in Ireland
(OS of Ireland 1:50,000 Sheet 16)

In *The Ley Hunter* no. 119 Paul Devereux first noted a straight fairy road, now visible as a motor road near Streedagh, in County Sligo in the Republic of Ireland. It starts at a *rath* or fairy fort (1) and travels in a dead straight line (2) for about a mile. If extended, the line of the road passes through two more *raths* at Arnaglass Lower (3) and Ardnalglass Bridge (4), heading in the general direction of the massive flat-topped Benbulbin mountain (5) in an area traditionally considered to be inhabited by fairies. Further investigation in the area by Gordon McLellan revealed another alignment in the same area running due east from another *rath* south of Streedagh (6). The line passes through two groups of fairy forts near Newtown and Kiltykere (7), and Gortaderry (8) and on to the summit of Benwisken (9), another peak close to Benbulbin. West of the *rath* and south of Streedagh, the alignment is marked by a straight track (10) that heads towards the beach, passing through a mound at Agharrow (11).

The fairy passes of Ireland display many of the characteristics that Watkins identified in his English leys – the alignment to prominent hills and mountains and the numerous legends of underground tunnels that run between *raths*, ring forts, castles or religious houses nearby, and they are often overlaid by fragments of roads and tracks. Add to that the tradition of fairies or spirits inhabiting fairy forts and travelling between them and you have the ingredients for a revival of ley hunting in the Emerald Isle.

'A SOLEMNE WALKE'
The Kennet Avenue at Avebury
(OS 1:50,000 Landranger Sheet 173)

When the antiquary William Stukeley wrote about the Avebury megaliths in the 18th century he interpreted the complex of huge standing stones as a gigantic serpent temple, the now lost Beckhampton Avenue being the tail, the henge and the stone circles its coiled body, and the Kennet Avenue and the Sanctuary on Overton Hill, the neck and head. Since these fanciful interpretations writers and archaeologists have referred to the remaining Kennet Avenue as 'sinuous'. It is not. Close inspection reveals that the two parallel lines of megaliths were built in discrete and *straight* sections over a long period of time. Furthermore, votive offerings and human burials were placed at the points where the Avenue changed direction and alongside the outer edges, thus confirming a connection between the lines and death rituals. The Sanctuary, a stone circle in Stukeley's time but now marked with concrete bollards, was previously a round timber mortuary house, like those at Stonehenge and Woodhenge, and was believed to have been used in funerary rites.

Today the avenue is largely a restoration and consists of two lines of evocatively shaped megaliths that define a sacred pathway between the Sanctuary and the Avebury henge. Archaeological investigations have revealed that people walked along the outsides of the avenue rather than between the rows of stones. Was that route preserved for the spirits of the dead?

THE SOUL'S JOURNEY
A shared funeral path
(OS 1:50,000 Landranger Sheet 172)

In *The Ley Hunter* no. 128, Phil Quinn noted two funeral paths that terminate at the village of Hawkesbury in South Gloucestershire, one linear, the other a circuit. The straight north–south path runs from Hillesley (**1**), two miles from Hawkesbury, and today can be followed along a public road to a crossroads (**2**) where the coffin was traditionally rested, prayers offered and psalms sung. The spot is also haunted by the spirits of monks from the time when the district was owned by Pershore Abbey. The locals call the place Coldchange Hill due to the sudden noticeable temperature drop as one descends the crossroads from the Cotswold scarp. The path continues as a footpath down to the church (**3**) on a route which mourners on the other, clockwise, funeral path from Kilcot (**5**) would use on their return journey. The two routes diverge at Coldchange Hill. On the Kilcot route the coffin was rested at a Neolithic long barrow (**4**).

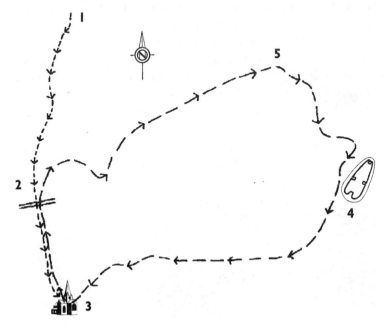

Hawkesbury funeral paths identified by Phil Quinn.

A SPANISH LEY
Parallel alignments
near Montserrat

First noted by the European ley hunter and artist John Palmer, this ley runs from San Miguel chapel (1) and is aligned on the summit of Tura de San Jeronimo (5), the highest peak in the Montserrat massif.

On its way it passes through Montserrat monastery (2). A chapel was erected at this site in AD 880 at the place where a revered 12th century image of the Virgin Mary apparently refused to move during an attempt by the Bishop of Vic to remove it to Manresa from its hiding place in the mountains. This strange phenomenon was considered a sign and a church was subsequently founded there. It was replaced in AD 976 by a Benedictine convent, which was later sacked by the French in the Peninsular War. The present building is modern.

Beyond the monastery the line takes in the church of San Antonio (3) and the hermitage of Ermita San Jeronimo (4) on its way to the mountain peak.

As an aside, Palmer notes a curious feature that is also associated with some English leys and some Bolivian straight tracks – that of the parallel alignment; a line drawn through the nearby chapels of Santa Cecilia and Los Apostles runs parallel to the Montserrat ley.

SPEYER CATHEDRAL LEY
German medieval geomancy

This German ley, in Palatinate, first noted by the ley researcher Ulrich Magin and now marked by medieval buildings, may have had its origins in prehistory as Palatinate was once thick with menhirs.

The ley runs due east–west and is aligned on the Kalmit mountain (**8**), the highest peak in Palatinate. It starts in the east as Speyer cathedral (**1**). This site has been in use as a sacred place for at least 2,000 years – the Romans referred to it as Civitas Nementum (deriving from the Celtic nemet, meaning sacred or holy place). The present cathedral dates from 1061, but there has been a church there since AD 360. Before that it was the site of a pagan Roman temple dedicated to the Celtic goddess Nantosvelta.

A straight road (**2**), following the alignment, connects the cathedral with the city gate (**3**), which dates from the 13th century. Onwards the ley passes over Dudenhofen church (**4**), Hanhofen church (**5**) and on to Hanhofen Castle (**6**), the site now only preserved by the moat that once surrounded it.

The next site is an old crossroads (**7**) of indeterminate date, but one of the roads is referred to as Hohlweg, similar to hollow (sunken) roads that are found in Britain, which could mean the crossing is at least medieval.

Finally, the ley terminates at Kalmit (**8**), a rocky peak that has no known sacred associations, but acts in the same way as one of Watkins's initial points.

STANTON DREW
Lines and leys in Somerset
(OS 1:50,000 Landranger Sheet 172)

In the village of Stanton Drew in Somerset, six miles south of Bristol, lies one of Britain's little known megalithic sites. It consists of three stone circles, the Great Circle being the third largest ring of stones in England (368ft in diameter), two stone avenues, a Cove and an outlying standing stone.

There are three alignments here. A line drawn through the centre of the south-western circle (**1**), through the centre of the Great Circle (**2**) passes over the now fallen Hautville's Quoit (**3**) and points to the place on the horizon where the midsummer sun rose in 2000 BC (**4**). Another line drawn from the centre of the north-eastern circle (**5**) and through the middle of the Great Circle passes through the Cove (**6**), a megalithic feature consisting of three upright stones and a capstone and points to the place on the horizon where the midwinter sun would have set when the stones were erected (**7**). The third alignment was noted by Alfred Watkins and joins all three circles with a line drawn tangentially to each of the circles, an alignment feature of stone circles he frequently noticed. Unknown to Watkins this line points towards the southernmost moonset (**8**).

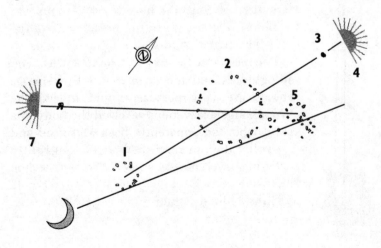

STONEHENGE CURSUS LEY
A prehistoric death road?
(OS 1:50,000 Landranger Sheet 184)

Often missed by casual visitors to Stonehenge is the cursus, a two-mile long rectangular earthen ditched enclosure that lies about half a mile north of Stonehenge itself. The antiquary William Stukeley first noticed it in 1723 when he interpreted it as a Roman racecourse, hence the name cursus. It is one of many such Neolithic monuments, but none of them were racecourses. Another, the Dorset cursus, has been described by the archaeologist Richard Bradley as an 'avenue of the dead'.

The Stonehenge cursus (2) links a group of round barrows at its western end (1) to a long barrow (3) at its eastern extremity. Alfred Watkins first noted that a line drawn along the straight northern ditch passes through the Cuckoo Stone (4) to the east, a standing stone not marked on the 1:50,000 map. Excavations by Mrs Cunnington in the 1930s revealed the circular henge monument now called Woodhenge (5) and to his delight Watkins was able to extend his ley through the centre of the site. This alignment was later given archaeological credence in 1947. The links between straightness and the dead at the Stonehenge cursus are very persuasive and indeed the Woodhenge excavations revealed the body of a child who had apparently been sacrificed and buried at the centre of the henge.

Paul Devereux has since extended the line further east to where it strikes the horizon at Beacon Hill (6), thus finding its Watkinsian terminal point.

A SUNRISE LINE
An astronomical alignment at Stonehenge
(OS 1:50,000 Landranger Sheet 184)

Perhaps the most famous of all ancient astronomical alignments is the summer solstice alignment at Stonehenge, Wiltshire. On the longest day of the year, viewed from the centre of the monument, the sun can be seen rising over the outlying Heel Stone (**4**) between the massive uprights that form the central ring (**3**). The earth-banked Avenue (**5**) that leads away from Stonehenge is aligned in the same direction for several hundred yards.

The antiquary William Stukeley first noted this strange phenomenon in 1740 when he wrote that the axis of Stonehenge and the Avenue are directed to the north-east 'whereabouts the sun rises when the days are longest'.

In *The Old Straight Track* Alfred Watkins notes that the alignment passes through two Bronze Age barrows (**1, 2**) to the south-west of Stonehenge. Stukeley noted another barrow (**6**) once visible on the skyline and lining up with the Avenue, marking the point on the horizon where the summer solstice sun would rise.

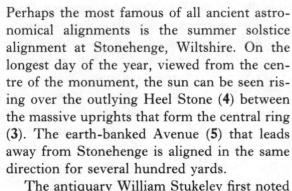

The back Prospect of the beginning of the Avenue to Stonehenge. 6 Aug. 1723.

William Stukeley's engraving of the Avenue as it stretches away from Stonehenge, aligned on the summer solstice sunrise, once marked by a barrow.

A SUPERNATURAL HIGHWAY
The spirit flight of Molly N
(OS 1:50,000 Landranger Sheet 172)

There is a folk tale attached to a length of the old coach road from Bristol to Wells that runs between Bedminster Down and East Harptree, suggesting that the route has a corresponding equivalent in the Otherworld. A tale related by Phil Quinn in *The Ley Hunter* no. 126 concerns the journey of an eccentric 19th century woman, Molly N, and a phantom horse. Exhausted on her journey from Bristol market she called out for a horse. A white pony appeared and carried her at a furious pace towards East Harptree. At the Mollybrook stream the horse stopped suddenly and threw her to the ground, knocking her unconscious.

The route followed by this 'spirit flight' is host to hauntings, holy wells, a stone circle, a corpse path and a suicide crossroads burial. The spirit path starts at the Cross Keys Inn (**1**), once the site of an 18th century gibbet, where the spectral horse appeared. It then passes a haunted driveway to Bishopsworth manor house (**2**), a haunted stretch of road over Dundry Hill (**3**), the ancient spring of Wriggleswell (**4**), and the foot of Pagan Hill (**5**), the site of a Roman temple and votive well. At Chew Stoke the road was once part of a burial path called Pilgrim's Way (**6**) which ran to St Andrew's church (**7**). A stone circle (**8**) once stood by the side of the road a few hundred yards further on, alongside a holy well (**9**). A modern diversion in the road misses Moreton Cross and St Mary's well (**10**) before rejoining the route at White Cross, a suicide burial place (**11**), and terminating at the parish boundary (**12**) where Molly N ended her spirit journey.

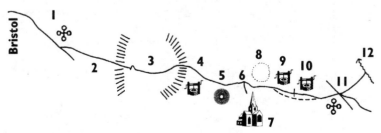

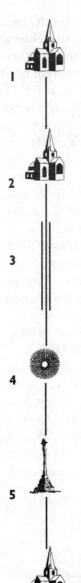

SUTTON WALLS LEY
A ghostly track revealed
(OS 1:50,000 Landranger Sheet 149)

This ley is given in *The Old Straight Track* and is an example of a map ley that is later corroborated by anecdotal information. This Herefordshire ley links Wellington church (**1**), Marden church (**2**), the Iron Age hill fort of Sutton Walls and a churchyard cross at Sutton St Nicholas church (**5**). The ley actually passes through a visible 'notch' on the edge of Sutton Walls ramparts, and an outlying mound (**4**). From this point the spire of Marden church and the tower of Wellington church can be seen in clear alignment. To the south-east the alignment ends at Western Beggard church (**6**).

A year after finding this alignment Watkins was approached by the owner of Sutton Walls who told him that ploughing had revealed an ancient track, as a dark mark in the field, running up to the mound at the edge of the camp along the line of the ley (**3**).

Veteran ley hunter Paul Devereux suggests that this old track might have been a medieval spirit way because when projected to the south-east the line would have passed through Sutton St Nicholas burial ground rather than the church itself.

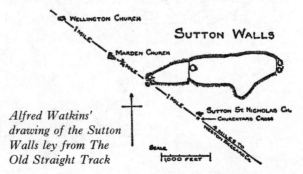

Alfred Watkins' drawing of the Sutton Walls ley from The Old Straight Track

THREE DUTCH DEAD ROADS
Westerheide, Hilversum, Netherlands

Straight *Doodwegen*, or death roads, are still visible in parts of the Netherlands. John Palmer first brought these medieval roads to the attention of ley hunters in 1989, though their real significance to ley hunting did not become apparent until three years later.

This splendid example comes from Westerheide (heath) between Laren (**2**) and Hilversum (**1**), in north Holland, an area dotted with Bronze Age barrows. Three dead straight *Doodwegen* converge on the isolated St Janskerhof (St John's cemetery) (**3**). The three roads are equally spaced forming a triangle pointing at the chapel of St John (**4**). The present day chapel is only a century old, but it replaced an earlier building said to date from the 1600s or earlier.

The death road from the village of 's-Graveland (**7**) is believed to have been laid out in 1643. The other two, from the villages of Bussum (**6**) and Ankerveen (**5**) are of uncertain date but are believed to be older. They are not Roman.

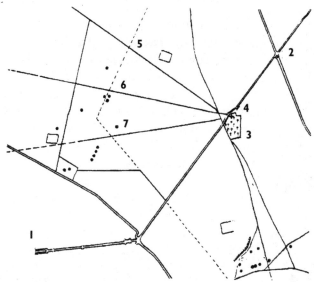

The Westerheide death roads, based on a map by John Palmer.

A TOR GUIDE
Glastonbury leys
(OS 1:50,000 Landranger Sheet 182)

Glastonbury is an unremarkable market town lying in the Somerset levels that has been associated with the earliest days of Christianity in Britain, with King Arthur and, which more recently, has become a magnet for New Age pilgrims. Several leys have been suggested passing through either the Tor or the Abbey ruins, both sites having attracted considerable mystical and religious significance.

The first ley was proposed by John Michell and lies on the axis of Glastonbury Abbey. This line points towards Stonehenge and includes St Benedict's church to the west; to the east the ley is preserved in the line of Dod Lane. Projected further east the line passes over St Michael's church on Gare Hill, the crossing point of several other leys, and then onwards to Stonehenge.

The second ley was proposed by Paul Devereux and Ian Thompson and links the 13th century St Nicholas's church at Brockley (**1**), with its tale of ghosts and subterranean tunnels, to Holy Trinity church at Burrington (**2**), to Gorsey Bigbury henge (**3**), and to Westbury Beacon Camp (**4**) on the Mendips and overlooking Glastonbury. The line then passes through a crossroads and possible markstone at Yarley (**5**) before meeting the Tor (**6**) with the ruined St Michael's church at the summit. The final marker is St Leonard's church at Butleigh (**7**) with possible Saxon origins. Coincidentally, Butleigh lies near the centre of the famous Glastonbury landscape Zodiac, claimed by Katherine Maltwood to have been etched into the landscape in the distant past.

TWO IRISH LEYS
A sunrise line and a classic ley at Lough Gur

(OS of Ireland Discovery Series Sheet 65)

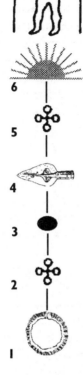

Lough Gur in County Limerick is at the centre of one of the greatest concentrations of prehistoric remains in the whole of Ireland. Two alignments have been noted in the vicinity of the lough. In *Mythic Ireland*, Michael Dames describes a Lammas sunrise line starting at Rannach Croim Duibh (**1**), Ireland's largest stone circle (also known as the Lios). The Lammas sunrise (**6**) can be witnessed from the centre of the circle through the upright entrance stones. The sunrise line passes through a Neolithic stone platform on an artificial island of boulders in the lake (**2**), across Suideachan, a flat topped stone slab, and in legend the Birth Chair of the Celtic harvest goddess Aine (**3**), over the presumed site of votive offerings, where a Bronze Age gold spear was unearthed in 1857 (**4**), and finally to Money Hole (**5**), traditionally believed to be the site of a mythic crock of gold.

The second alignment is of a more conventionally Watkinsian nature and was first noted by Chris Castle in *The Ley Hunter* in 1976. It links a smaller stone circle (**7**), to the north of the Lios, a massive squared standing stone called the Pillar Stone (**8**), across an intervening ridge and through an unnamed long mound with a large stone half buried in its side (**9**) and thence on to the prominent unexcavated stone fort (**10**) on Knockfennel, a prominent hill and a classic Watkins 'initial point'. The alignment was originally noted by Sir Norman Lockyer, who suggested that the line was directed to the ancient rising points of stars.

UFFINGTON LEY
A dragon and a holy hill
(OS 1:50,000 Landranger Sheet 174)

The Ridgeway has been described as the oldest road in England. It snakes its way across the ridges of hills from the Thames at Streatley to Salisbury Plain, on route passing the oldest known chalk hill figure in the country, the White Horse of Uffington. Above the figure on the top of White Horse Hill is an Iron Age earthwork which is a contender for a 'holy hill' in this alignment, which was first noted by Paul Devereux and Ian Thompson in *The Ley Hunter's Companion*.

The alignment runs for nearly 10 miles and commences at the 13th century church of St Mary's at Uffington, Oxfordshire (1). From here the line rises up the escarpment to pass over Dragon Hill (2), a natural conical hill with an artificially flattened top. The grass never grows on the summit because according to local legend, it was here that St George killed the dragon. Where its blood fell nothing would grow. Further up the steep slope is the third marker point, a Bronze Age barrow (3). The Iron Age Uffington Castle camp (4) lies on the top of the hill at the highest point of the Berkshire Downs. The alignment continues beyond the camp and was probably designed to point towards the hilltop as well. The other end of the ley is marked by a tumulus (8) east of Preston. It then passes over two linear earthworks at Farncombe Down (7) and Near Down (6), where the ley is marked by a gap in the bank, to another tumulus on Parkfarm Down (5), terminating at White Horse Hill.

WILMINGTON LEY
A long man and a holy hill
(OS 1:50,000 Landranger Sheet 199)

5

4

Alfred Watkins deduced from place name evidence that his proposed Stone Age ley surveyors were probably called 'dod' men. Looking for illustrations of potential ancient surveyors he seized upon the ancient chalk hill figure of the Long Man of Wilmington as a representation of the ley man. It is fitting therefore that the Long Man should lie on a ley, and a holy hill at that.

This ley was first noted by Paul Devereux and Ian Thompson in *The Ley Hunter's Companion* and runs for two miles in roughly north–south direction.

The first ley marker is St Mary's and St Peter's church (**1**) in the village of Wilmington, Sussex, a 12th century building which legend says is connected to the crypt of the next ley point, Wilmington Priory (**2**). Legends of underground tunnels often crop up on leys. The priory, of the Benedictine persuasion, was founded in Norman times.

3

The third marker is the Long Man (**3**), a 237ft long, featureless outline of a human figure holding a long staff in each hand (Watkins' surveyor's staffs). The outline is today marked with bricks, laid when the figure was re-cut in the 19th century. The date of the Long Man is uncertain, but is possibly pre-Roman. The top of the hill on which the Long Man lies is marked by the Windover Hill round barrow (**4**), 135ft in diameter and marking the holy hill. The line can be extended further north where it crosses a hard-to-find Bronze Age bowl barrow (**5**).

2

1

WINCHESTER LEY
Holy hill and straight walking
(OS 1:50 000, Landranger Sheet 185)

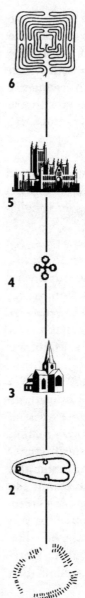

In *The Ley Hunter's Companion*, Paul Devereux and Ian Thompson describe this ley that runs in a roughly north–south direction for nearly 12 miles. Centred on St Catherine's Hill outside Winchester in Hampshire, the ley commences at Tidbury Ring (**1**), an Iron Age camp, bisects the remains of a Neolithic long barrow (**2**) near south Wonston before entering Winchester at St Bartholomew's church (**3**), a 12th-century building. The line continues across the road and passes through the 15th-century Hyde Gate (**4**) at the site of Hyde Abbey, where tradition has it Alfred the Great is buried. The next point is Winchester Cathedral (**5**), a Norman building on the site of an earlier Saxon foundation and possibly the site of a megalithic structure. The ley then leaves Winchester on route to St Catherine's Hill. The hill is crowned with an Iron Age earthwork in which the medieval St Catherine's chapel once stood. The ley itself actually passes through a turf labyrinth known as the Mizmaze (**6**). Such labyrinths have a long pedigree and were associated in Christian symbolism with the soul's journey to heaven. Their use as spirit traps in other cultures has been noted.

E.O. Gordon, 1932, recorded the tradition of a twice daily procession by 'seventy black gowned scholars' from Winchester College to the summit of the 'Holy Hill' (St Catherine's Hill). An engraving in *Prehistoric London* shows the scholars walking a straight path towards the hill. Perhaps this tradition of 'going to Hilles' retained a memory of the old straight track.

YAZOR LEY
Mark stones
(OS 1:50,000 Landranger Sheet 149)

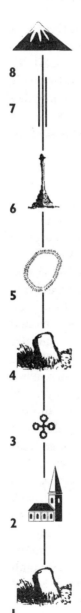

Alfred Watkins suggests that mark stones were planted near to sighting mounds to indicate the direction of a ley – in other words to provide an indication of the right direction with which to make a sighting. They were also frequently put at the crossing point of two leys, and are therefore sometimes to be found at present-day crossroads.

Watkins describes an example of a ley containing mark stones centred on Yazor in Herefordshire. He notes in *The Old Straight Track* a mark stone on the highway at Yazor church (**1**), the ruined tower of Yazor Old Church (**2**), Monnington Court (**3**), a mark stone on the highway at Wilmarston (**4**), a hill fort near Whitehouse Farm (**5**), a churchyard cross at Capel-y-Ffin in Monmouthshire (**6**), which Watkins suspected evolved from a former mark stone, a bridle pass over Tarenyr-Esgob (**7**) terminating on the Black Mountain peak of Pen-y-Gader (**8**).

Shortly before going to press with *The Old Straight Track*, Watkins observed that a mark stone in a clump of trees on high ground at Mansel Gamage that had been shown to him by the estate owner Sir John Cotterill sometime earlier, also fell on this ley. Standing at the ruins of Old Yazor Church the clump can be seen in direct alignment with Pen-y-Gader. As he was in the process of photographing this alignment his companion noticed a mark stone in the highway hedge three yards away. Watkins's photographs of this ley are included in *The Ley Hunter's Manual*.

YORK MINSTER LEY
A medieval church alignment
(OS 1:50,000 Landranger Sheet 105)

Documentary evidence for medieval church alignment practice is hard to find, but there are several examples of what appears to be the deliberate alignment of ancient churches in some of Britain's old cities. This example, first noted by Brian Larkman, connects seven ancient religious structures in a straight line 2,745ft long.

Situated within the city walls of York and passing through the geomantic centre of the city is the York Minster ley. This alignment is spectacularly visible from the tower of York Minster. The best way to walk the ley is from its starting point, a spit of land between the Foss and Ouse rivers. This was once Templar land. The line passes through the site of St George's chapel (1), a Templar building, and continues through the Norman castle, Clifford's Tower (2) with its 11th century chapel, on to the spired church of St Mary's (3), dating from the 11th century and now York Heritage Centre, on to the 15th century All Saints Pavement (4), a church built on the site of earlier 11th and 7th century churches. All Saints is the oldest church on the line and sits at the crossroads at the centre of the city. The next site along the line is the 14th century St Samson's church (5), now a senior citizen's centre. The next site is the Minster itself, St Peter's Cathedral (6). The ley passes directly below the 11th century tower at the crossing of the nave and transepts. The line terminates at the 13th century Archbishop's Palace chapel (7), but is inaccessible to the public.

INDEX